Religious Education, Parish and Youth Ministry

Legal Issues for Catechetical and Youth Leaders

Mary Angela Shaughnessy,
SCN, J.D., Ph.D.

NATIONAL CATHOLIC
EDUCATIONAL ASSOCIATION

Second Printing 2008
Part No. REL–24–1368
ISBN 1–55833–381–9

Dedication

KARL RAHNER once wrote:

The priest is not an angel sent from heaven,
He is a man chosen from among men,
a member of the Church, a Christian.

Remaining man and Christian,
He begins to speak to you the word of God.
The word is not his own.
No. He comes to you because God has
told him to proclaim God's Word.

For must not some one of us say something about God,
About eternal life,
About the majesty of God in our sanctified being;
Must not some one of us speak of sin, the judgment,
The mercy of God?

So, my dear friends, pray for him.
Carry him
so that he might be able to sustain others
by bringing them the mystery
of God's love revealed in Jesus Christ.

With a grateful heart, I dedicate this book to

REVEREND MICHAEL L. HUGGINS
Priest, healer, teacher, friend, brother
Who is not afraid to speak the truth in love,
A true *alter Christus.*
The Church and world are better places
Because he is here.
I am blessed to call him friend and brother.

— Mary Angela Shaughnessy, SCN
January, 2006

Table of Contents

Acknowledgments

FOR THE PAST EIGHTEEN YEARS, the National Catholic Educational Association has generously provided me a forum from which to share my ideas and research on the topic of civil law and its relationship to the many educational and faith formation ministries of the Catholic Church. I am deeply grateful for the faith the organization has shown in my work and in me.

Eleven years ago I first ventured into the field of religious education and the law; I also wrote texts on youth ministry and campus ministry. Each one has been a labor of love and a true joy. I am very grateful to Diana Dudoit Raiche who encouraged the writing of this text and provided assistance and advice.

I thank my more than capable assistant, Mrs. Joan Danner, who manages to keep everything organized for me, even on the busiest of days.

I thank the countless people who have attended my seminars and workshops, who have written and called me, and who have shared with me their legal and ethical struggles. They, the people who labor in the field, are the true heros and heroines of education and ministry.

I thank my family, especially the next generation, whose years in Catholic education in its various forms continue to provide me with inspiration for my writing. I thank my religious community, the Sisters of Charity of Nazareth, who have been unfailing in their support of my ministry.

I thank my dear friend, Dr. Karen Juliano, President of Notre Dame Academy in Tyngsboro, Massachusetts, for her unfailing support and belief in me even on those days when I find it hard to believe in myself. I thank Father Michael Huggins, my good friend and colleague, who is never too busy to answer thorny questions, help me navigate issues of Canon Law and Church practice, and pray with me.

Two schools generously allowed me to use part of their policy statements in this text and I am very grateful. I thank Providence High School in Burbank, California and Catholic Memorial High School in the Archdiocese of Boston for permission to use their work.

Finally, I thank you, the reader. May this text make a small contribution to your educational ministry in the Catholic Church.

— Mary Angela Shaughnessy, SCN
January, 2006

Preface

ONCE AGAIN Sr. Mary Angela Shaughnessy, SCN has provided those who labor on behalf of the Gospel in parish-based catechetical settings a valuable resource for understanding the legal landscape associated with educational and pastoral ministry. As a Sister of Charity of Nazareth with advanced degrees in both legal and educational administration, she is well qualified to educate catechetical leaders in parishes, youth ministry and schools about current law as it pertains to ministry. In this volume for leaders and its companion for volunteers she has updated her previous two books for those same audiences on religious education and the law.

I am most grateful to Sr. Mary Angela for equipping catechetical leaders in the field to serve with greater competence in various positions of responsibility through these books. Special thanks also goes to Robert J. McCarty, D.Min., executive director of the National Federation for Catholic Youth Ministry, for early consultation on the project. He and Michael Theisen of NFCYM gave valuable recommendations and served as readers for the project. I thank Kathy Schmitt, former youth and campus minister, for her valuable editorial assistance, Christina Gergits for assistance in managing the project, Steve Palmer for editorial assistance and Paul Serrano for design.

> Diana Dudoit Raiche
> Executive Director
> Department of Religious Education

Chapter One

Introduction

TEN YEARS HAVE PASSED since the appearance of the text, *Religious Education and the Law: A Handbook for Catechetical Directors* and its companion volume, *Religious Education and the Law: A Catechist Handbook*. Although a number of texts had been written specifically for Catholic schools, these texts were the first that were devoted to legal challenges facing those who ministered in the field of religious education. Much has happened since 1996. Nothing has been more dramatic than the sexual abuse crisis that has catapulted our Church into a legal, ethical and moral morass. This crisis has saddened and disheartened the faithful, and made many who minister in the Church fearful of both their ministry and the legal system.

The sexual abuse crisis is not the only issue that has arisen in the past ten years. The explosion of technology has created new challenges and risks. Adults no longer communicate with each other and with minors only in person and in writing; e-mail has become both convenient and problematic. Expectations of privacy have eroded. September 11, 2001, brought the country face-to-face with our human vulnerability and forced us to examine possibilities virtually beyond our comprehension in the immediate past. Parishes and schools, for example, that had outlawed cell phones had to confront the possibility that a cell phone might enable a young person to have a last conversation with a doomed loved-one. As new issues emerge, policies and procedures must change.

This new text, *Religious Education, Parish and Youth Ministry: Legal Issues for the Catechetical Leader*, expands the scope of the previous text to include campus and youth ministers as well as religious educators, all of whom are catechetical leaders. It includes topics either not discussed or lightly treated in the earlier text including: boundaries, harassment, hazing and bullying, the Internet, e-mail, health and medication issues, violence, special needs, and other issues. Certainly, the horizon of legal issues in religious education and ministry has widened.

Chapter I presents a pre-test that offers readers the opportunity to assess their degree of legal knowledge. After one has taken the test, one can "correct" it and read the explanations for the answers.

Chapter II offers an overview of law as it affects ministry to, and education of, young persons. Both civil law and Canon Law, the law of the Church, are discussed. In order to understand civil law as it impacts Church ministry, it is necessary to spend some time considering the law that impacts the public sector and government operations. The reader may be surprised to learn that, despite some real differences, there are many similarities.

Chapter III discusses tort law, particularly the law of negligence, which is the most often litigated tort. If a religious educator or minister is sued for any action or inaction, there is a strong likelihood that the allegation will be one of negligence. This fact may surprise many who mistakenly believe that sexual abuse is the most-often litigated wrong. Simple negligence cases rarely constitute front-page news; nonetheless, these cases are, by far, the most often litigated. This chapter will discuss a wide range of issues, including abuse, privacy, off-site activities, adult/minor relationships, e-mail and other technology—all with a view to prevention of problems and lawsuits. It is far easier to stay out of court and avoid a lawsuit than it is to defend and win one that could have been avoided.

Chapter IV discusses the rights and responsibilities of bishops, parishes, pastors, councils and boards, as well as the types of boards governing or advising those who administer religious education and youth or campus ministry programs.

Chapter V discusses the supervision of parish/program/school staff and volunteers.

Chapter VI offers some insights into the rights and responsibilities of parents and young people.

The rights and responsibilities of parish/program/school staff, including paid staff and volunteers, are discussed in Chapter VII. The topic of fidelity to Church teaching is also addressed.

Chapter VIII presents some final reflections and recommendations for "lawful" ministry.

You are invited to turn the page and take the twenty question pre-test.

Legal Pre-Test for Religious Education and Ministry:

How Much Do You Already Know?

Please answer *True* or *False*.

_____ 1. Adults and young persons in Catholic parishes and programs have the same Constitutional protections as those in public and government-sponsored programs.

_____ 2. After ensuring safety, catechetical leaders or youth/campus ministers' first legal responsibility is to be true to the teachings of the Catholic Church.

_____ 3. It is never legally permissible to leave students under the age of 18 unattended.

_____ 4. Persons should be told what it is they have done "wrong" and allowed to present their side(s) of the story before penalties are imposed.

_____ 5. If a young person is granted due process in disciplinary proceedings, he or she must also be allowed to bring legal Counsel to any internal proceedings.

_____ 6. If an adult supervisor believes that a catechetist, youth or campus minister, volunteer or student is a troublemaker, that belief should be noted in writing.

_____ 7. If parents have signed a field trip release form, the parish or school cannot be held liable for any injuries that occur.

_____ 8. The Americans with Disabilities Act requires that all persons with disabilities must be allowed to participate in programs and the parish must provide any needed accommodation.

_____ 9. A catechetical leader, youth or campus minister can be held liable for the actions or omissions of those under his or her supervision.

_____ 10. Every person who volunteers in a parish or program must be screened.

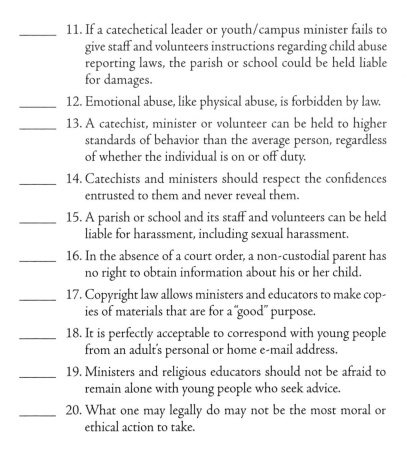

_____ 11. If a catechetical leader or youth/campus minister fails to give staff and volunteers instructions regarding child abuse reporting laws, the parish or school could be held liable for damages.

_____ 12. Emotional abuse, like physical abuse, is forbidden by law.

_____ 13. A catechist, minister or volunteer can be held to higher standards of behavior than the average person, regardless of whether the individual is on or off duty.

_____ 14. Catechists and ministers should respect the confidences entrusted to them and never reveal them.

_____ 15. A parish or school and its staff and volunteers can be held liable for harassment, including sexual harassment.

_____ 16. In the absence of a court order, a non-custodial parent has no right to obtain information about his or her child.

_____ 17. Copyright law allows ministers and educators to make copies of materials that are for a "good" purpose.

_____ 18. It is perfectly acceptable to correspond with young people from an adult's personal or home e-mail address.

_____ 19. Ministers and religious educators should not be afraid to remain alone with young people who seek advice.

_____ 20. What one may legally do may not be the most moral or ethical action to take.

Answers and Discussion

1. *Adults and young persons in Catholic parishes, schools and programs have the same Constitutional protections as those in public schools and government-sponsored programs.* **FALSE.**

The vast majority of people encountering this statement for the first time will choose "true" as the correct answer. It sounds as if it should be true. After all, doesn't everyone have Constitutional rights? Isn't that what the founding fathers established? The answer is that the United States government guarantees that it and its agents will protect the Constitutional rights of all persons in their institutions and programs. The Constitution is completely silent as to what private institutions and their agents may do, and leaves any such regulation of private activity to the state and its legislatures. For example, the First Amendment to the United States Constitution states, "Congress shall make no law respecting an establishment of religion ..." The founders of this country sought to ensure that there would never be a state religion and that individuals would not be compelled to abandon their personal religious beliefs.

Government operations, such as the police and fire departments, are state agencies and those who staff them must recognize and respect the Constitutional rights of both citizens and those who work in the government. A Catholic school or parish program may have rules and regulations that the public school may not have. Private institutions have no obligation to respect and protect Constitutional rights. They have moral and ethical obligations, of course, and the law expects them to treat people fairly, according to the legal principle of "good faith and fair dealing," but private institutions can restrict and even forbid behaviors that public institutions and programs have to allow. For example, a Catholic hospital can forbid employees to express opinions contrary to the teachings of the Catholic Church. An employee could be prohibited from participating in a public rally in support of gay marriage and sanctioned if he or she chose to participate in spite of the prohibition. A public hospital or one operated by a state university could not impose such restrictions on its employees because the First Amendment guarantees free speech to those in its institutions.

2. *After ensuring safety, catechetical leaders or youth/campus ministsers' first legal responsibility is to be true to the teaching of the Catholic Church.* **TRUE**

Religious education and youth/campus ministry programs exist to promote the Catholic Church, to teach the tenets of the Church and to provide a community where young people can examine and test their beliefs and practice their faith. There really is no other reason to offer such programs. Social service agencies provide community service offerings. The YMCA, scouts and other service organizations provide places to "stay out of trouble," practice citizenship and do good deeds. Jesus Christ founded the Catholic Church and those who serve in any capacity should be true to its teachings. Certainly, not every Catholic absolutely accepts unquestioningly everything the Church teaches. But religious education and youth/campus ministry programs are not the places for adults to share doubts, criticize the Church, or try to work out their personal issues with the Church.

Some parents, unfortunately, may place their children in religious education programs so that they can participate in "rites of passage" such as First Penance, First Communion and Confirmation, rather than for a strong foundation in the Catholic faith. Some young people may choose youth ministry and campus ministry programs for the social experiences. If fidelity to the teachings of the Catholic Church is not a commitment of those administering and working in religious education and youth ministry, there is no real reason for them to exist.

3. *It is never legally permissible to leave students under the age of 18 unattended.* **FALSE.**

Anyone reading this text who has ever worked in a school or religious education program can probably recall a principal or other supervisor firmly advising that students are "never to be left unattended." Indeed, such was the prevailing wisdom. Yet it would probably be difficult to find even one teacher or catechist who could honestly say that he or she has never left young persons unattended. It is legally incorrect to tell adult supervisors that they can "never" leave young persons unattended. There are circumstances in which the prudent action is to leave young persons unattended. If a catechist really needs to use the restroom, for example, he or she may leave students unattended for a reasonable amount of time. In the case of an emergency, a term for which courts have not provided a definition, young people can also be left unattended.

One story comes from my years as a high school principal teaching one English class. During class one morning, three students hurriedly entered the room stating, "Sister, you have to come quick!! Kathy has her arm caught in the Kotex machine in the bathroom and it is turning blue." There are no written policies dealing with just such a situation. But a reasonable person would leave the students in the classroom unattended and go to the bathroom and try to extricate the student from the machine—which is what I did. Having no success and unable to locate a janitor, I called the Fire Department who came and released the student's arm from the machine. No reasonable teacher would wait to help Kathy until some adult could come to cover the class. Emergencies demand immediate responses. Indeed, failure to respond in a timely manner could well constitute legal negligence if a student should sustain further injury as a result of the failure to act.

Should a student/participant be injured while the catechist or youth/campus minister was out of the room or area, the court would apply the "reasonable person" test. Did the catechist or youth/campus minister act the way one would expect a reasonably prudent person to act? If a catechist or youth/campus minister learns that an emergency exists nearby and no other adult can be summoned, the reasonable person would leave the young people unattended and go deal with the emergency. If a student in the classroom is injured in the absence of the catechist or youth/campus minister, that person may, as indicated above, avoid liability if the judge and/or jury find the actions reasonable, in the light of all the circumstances.

Courts do expect that supervising adults will have told young persons what the expectations are if the adult has to leave them without supervision. At a minimum, young people should be instructed to remain in their seats and work quietly or to cease athletic play or other activity. Many religious education or youth/campus ministry rooms can display posted rules and one rule might be, "If no adult is in the room, students will remain seated." Of course, one has to give age appropriate directions.

Courts expect that adults will take the age of those under their supervision into consideration when absenting themselves from their classrooms or areas. The principle, "the younger the child chronologically or mentally, the greater the standard of care," will generally govern the situation. More latitude can be afforded the actions of a supervisor of eighth-graders or high school students than one who supervises preschool or kindergarten students.

4. *Persons should be told what it is they have done "wrong" and allowed to present their side(s) of the story before penalties are imposed.* **TRUE.**

Religious education and youth/campus ministry programs may be less structured, at least in some ways, than "regular" classrooms. Catechists and youth/campus ministers certainly spend less time with young people than do those who teach them in schools. A reasonable adult who is striving to be fair in dealings with a young person will want to take the time to listen to his or her version of a story before disciplining the individual. The reality, however, may well be that the harried catechist or youth/campus minister who has just watched the student commit an infraction does not see any need for listening to a "story." Yet, things are not always what they seem. Maybe John did punch Joe, but did Joe do something to provoke John? Provocation will not excuse John, but it might mitigate the punishment. Most people have had the experience of being absolutely convinced that someone under his or her supervision did something that was wrong only to discover later that the conviction was a mistaken one. Perhaps closer to home, most people will recall at least one time when adults accused them of doing something they did not do, and the adult would not listen. Every educator and minister who wishes to be fair will take the time, even if it seems a "waste of time," to listen to an accused person's story.

In the public sector, this listening to someone's side of a story is called *procedural due process* and is guaranteed by the United States Constitution. While the religious educator or minister is not bound by all nine requirements of Constitutional procedural due process, he or she is expected to be "fair" and to follow the first three elements of procedural due process, which constitute the requirements for "good faith and fair dealing" which does bind everyone: (1) *notice* and (2) *a hearing* (3) *before an impartial tribunal.*

5. *If a young person is granted due process in disciplinary proceedings, he or she must also be allowed to bring legal counsel to any internal proceedings.* **FALSE.**

The right to representation by counsel is a Constitutional one, guaranteed by the Fifth and Fourteenth Amendments to the United States Constitution. However, there is no right to legal representation in the internal proceedings of private institutions.

The presence of attorneys at non-judicial proceedings poses problems. If the accused is allowed to bring an attorney to a hearing, then the parish or school will have to be represented by an attorney who attends the proceedings. If two attorneys are present during disciplinary hearings, the situation may quickly become adversarial and any hope of reconciliation may disappear. Parishes and schools are not courtrooms and administrators have a right to determine who will be present at such hearings. Parents, of course, should always be welcomed at hearings, if they wish to attend.

6. *If an adult supervisor believes that a catechetist, youth or campus minister, volunteer or student is a troublemaker, that belief should be noted in writing.* **FALSE.**

Once something is in writing, it can be used in many ways, not the least of which is against the writer. Persons should be most careful in writing notes and opinions that involve or could involve the reputations of others. Most people probably grew up hearing a parent or other significant adult say something such as, "Don't put anything in writing that you would be ashamed to see on the front page of the paper." Anything that is not protected by privilege, such as attorney/client, is "discoverable" and the writer or institution can be required to produce it in hearings or trials where the meaning can be open to more than one interpretation.

The law of defamation of character governs written statements. Whatever is written should follow three rules: (1) it should be specific; (2) it should be behaviorally-oriented; and (3) it should be verifiable. "Troublemaker" is not a specific term. What one person may deem behavior making a student a "troublemaker," another person may find praiseworthy.

Before committing any statements to writing, the writer should ask, "Is it necessary or important that I write this?" If the answer is "yes," then write a statement that is specific, behaviorally-oriented and verifiable.

The law of defamation governs situations involving what one person says or writes about another that may affect a person's reputation when heard or read by a third party. There are two types of defamation: slander, which is spoken, and libel, which is written. Obviously, libel is easier to prove than slander because of the existence of a written document.

7. *If parents have signed a field trip release form, the parish or school cannot be held liable for any injuries that do occur.* **FALSE.**

The correct response to this statement is "false" because parents and guardians cannot "sign away" their children's right to safety nor absolve supervisors of the responsibility to take reasonable care of the minors they supervise. Educators, parents and lawyers have been discussing and arguing about field trips for years and it may appear that little could be left to say on the subject.

Field trips have long been part of the educational experience in schools. Parish religious education programs, campus and youth ministry programs often offer experiences away from the parish or school. Adults want young people to see that learning and service are not confined to churches and school buildings. Off-site experiences give children and adolescents the opportunity to apply knowledge to "real life" situations. However, off-site trips carry special liability issues which will be discussed in the next chapter.

8. *The Americans with Disabilities Act requires that all persons with disabilities must be allowed to participate in programs and the parish must provide any needed accommodation.* **FALSE.**

No law, federal or state, requires that anyone allow any and all persons with disabilities to participate in any activity nor requires that an institution or program provide any needed accommodation. There is still some disagreement as to whether the ADA applies to religious institutions such as churches. However, most states have disability laws that do apply to religious institutions. Discrimination law requires that otherwise qualified individuals not be discriminated against on the basis of disability if, with reasonable accommodation, the individual can meet the program requirements. Regardless of whether the law requires it, a Catholic administrator or minister should act fairly. No one should be denied participation in a program or activity simply because his or her participation will be inconvenient for the supervisors. If, for example, a legally blind teenager wanted to enroll in religious education classes and the only accommodation needed was the ability to magnify materials, the accommodation should be made. Equally important, though, is the reality that no one has to go to unreasonable lengths to accommodate someone.

Students who have mental disabilities should also not be told that they cannot participate in an educational or ministerial program. A student with an IQ of 60 probably cannot meet the requirements of a Catholic school for admission, but could be part of a youth ministry group. Jesus has said, "Suffer the little children [big children, too] come unto me." He did not say, "Let only the normal ones come." No one is allowed to discriminate on the basis of disability. However, Catholic programs are not required to accept students with special needs. What religious educators and youth ministers need to keep in mind is really two-fold: what civil law requires and what the Gospel demands. Everyone in the Catholic Church has a right to access the services of the Church. Religious education and youth ministry are such services.

9. *A catechetical leader, youth or campus minister can be held liable for the actions or inactions of those under his or her supervision.* **TRUE.**

The legal doctrine of *respondeat superior*, let the superior answer, can hold superiors responsible for the actions of subordinates. If a catechist is absent from a classroom when a student is injured and a court deems the absence unreasonable, the supervisor can be held liable if it can be shown that he or she knew of the problem and took no measures to correct the situation.

Religious education, youth and campus ministry programs are far less structured than school programs. Students attend school five days a week; those in Church programs attend only a few hours a week. There is always the possibility for something to go wrong. Therefore, supervisors must exercise careful, prudent vigilance.

10. Every person who volunteers in a parish or program must be screened.
FALSE.

At this time (2006), the statement is legally false. Quite a number of states do not require that every volunteer in a parish be screened. The statement would be "true" if the word "should" were substituted for the word "must" as in "Every person who volunteers in a parish or program should be screened."

In light of the *Bishops' Charter on the Protection of Young People*, many dioceses are now mandating that persons who volunteer more than a single time in a parish, religious education program, youth or campus ministry program, or any program in which young persons will be present, be fingerprinted or otherwise screened. However, there are still situations in which screening has not been mandated. For example, if a mother comes to the religious education office, collects bookkeeping or typing work and takes it home to complete, some administrators would not screen the parent. However, a parent who routinely volunteers as an aide in a fourth-grade classroom would be screened. All volunteers should be screened, as it would be very easy for someone to change from a bookkeeping job to a religious education aide or youth ministry volunteer position and "fall through the cracks," as it were, and not be screened.

The day is not too far off when every parent who enrolls his or her child in any parish program will be screened. While this statement may sound extreme, Catholic parishes, programs and schools, can set such requirements. Some parents may find such a practice objectionable, but they should be helped to understand that the reason for it is the protection of children—theirs and all young people attending the programs. Parents should be informed that conviction of a crime is not an automatic bar to volunteering (much less barring the child's participation). If ten years ago a parent stole a car and was convicted but has lived an exemplary life since, the theft conviction should probably not keep the parent from volunteering. Obviously, some offenses are treated differently. A person with a conviction for child abuse should never be allowed to volunteer or have unsupervised contact with students. The risk is simply too great. Those with pedophile tendencies tend to gravitate toward programs with children or adolescents present. They may not seek employment if they have been convicted of a sexual crime because they know that the criminal record can easily be discovered, but they may seek to volunteer particularly in programs such as religious education and youth/campus ministry where they hope the level of scrutiny will be less.

11. *If a catechetical leader or youth/campus minister fails to give volunteer and paid staff instructions regarding child abuse reporting laws, the parish or school could be held liable for damages if a report of abuse is not made.* **TRUE.**

Under the doctrine of *respondeat superior* discussed above, the catechetical leader or youth/campus minister can be held liable for the actions or omissions of those they supervise. So, if an adult staff member violates state child abuse reporting laws by failing to report suspected child abuse, and if it can be shown that the catechetical leader or youth/campus minister never made the laws available to staff or volunteers, never referenced them in meetings, and had no policies and procedures regarding the reporting of abuse, liability can result.

One of the most serious issues confronting those involved in ministry with young people today is child abuse. Religious educators, youth ministers and campus ministers are in a particularly sensitive position. Young people often choose catechists or ministers as confidants in their struggles to deal with abuse and its effects. For this reason, boards of Catholic education, parish councils, pastors, parish catechetical leaders, campus/youth ministers and other staff must ensure that all employees and volunteers are as prepared as possible to deal with the realities of abuse and neglect. Parish and school leaders should consider adopting a policy such as, "This parish and school abide by the child abuse reporting statutes of the state." Further, policy should require that parish and school leaders spend some time reviewing pertinent state law, parish policies and school policies and providing information and discussion on the topic at one of the first staff meetings of the year. If a separate meeting is not provided for other employees and volunteers, such as secretaries, custodians and the like, the parish or school administrator should consider having them present for the appropriate portion of the staff meeting.

12. *Emotional abuse, like physical abuse, is forbidden by law.* **TRUE.**

Only a few years ago, emotional abuse was rarely, if ever, discussed. Social service agencies and police departments seemed to have their hands full dealing with sexual and physical abuse. Today, instances of emotional, psychological and mental abuse, as well as physical and sexual abuse, are being investigated. It is no longer rare, for example, for a teacher to be accused of emotional abuse, The topic of abuse will be discussed in greater detail in the next chapter.

13. *A catechist, minister or volunteer can be held to higher standards of behavior than the average person, regardless of whether the individual is on or off duty.* **TRUE.**

Some persons taking this pre-test may be surprised to learn that this statement is true. While people may readily concede that policies and procedures govern their behavior while they are working, they find it hard to believe that those same policies and procedures, as well as others, can govern their "off duty" behavior. A religious educator, youth or campus minister is a role model and, as such, has certain responsibilities. If a catechetical leader or youth minister is arrested for driving under the influence of alcohol, it is highly likely that the newspaper report will mention the individual's place of employment while, in similar circumstances, another person's place of employment might not be mentioned. The same is true of those who volunteer.

Catechetical leaders are often confronted with issues of actual or perceived inappropriate staff conduct, and may wonder what legal rights they have to demand certain standards of behavior from staff members, particularly during off-duty times. What a staff member does, both in and outside the educational or ministerial setting, impacts the quality and integrity of ministry within the setting. The doctrine of separation of church and state protects Catholic programs, parishes, schools, and their administrators and allows them to set standards of personal behavior that would not be permitted in the public sector.

There is no expectation that an administrator be the private morality police and intrude inappropriately into the private lives of others. But if what a person does violates Church teaching and becomes a source of scandal, administrators have a moral duty to act. In summary, then, once an individual performs an act that is inconsistent with Church teaching and becomes publicly known, that person may no longer be qualified to minister in a given situation at that time. While such expectations of morally-correct behavior for Church staff or volunteers may seem obvious, it is recommended that documents state the requirement of supporting the teachings of the Church and setting a high moral standard of behavior in private as well as in public.

14. *Catechists and ministers should respect the confidences entrusted to them and should never reveal them.* **FALSE.**

Most people have heard at least one story involving a teacher who received a student confidence, failed to act on the knowledge, and the student later harmed self or others. Some religious educators and ministers mistakenly believe that they are protected by "privilege," which allows them to keep information shared by young persons confidential. There really are only two privileges that are still recognized by courts in this country: priest/penitent and attorney/client. If a young person tells a catechist that he is thinking about killing himself and the catechist does not tell a parent or supervisor, and the student later kills himself, recent case law indicates that the individual who fails to report can be charged with negligent homicide and voluntary or involuntary manslaughter, all of which are crimes. All such cases to date have involved teachers in schools, but there is little doubt that the same reasoning could be applied to any adult in a supervisory situation involving minors.

While the topic of confidentiality will be discussed later in the text, adults should be aware at the onset that young persons should be told in age-appropriate language, "I will keep your confidence so long as no one's life, health, or safety is involved. Once they are involved, there is no confidentiality."

15. *A parish or school and its staff and volunteers can be held liable for harassment, including sexual harassment.* **TRUE.**

Supervisors, as well as institutions or programs, can be held liable for harassment committed by others if they knew about it and took no action or if they should have known about it. They will not be held liable for harassment of which they had no knowledge and for which there was no reasonable expectation that they should have known about it.

There is, of course, harassment that consists of behavior that is annoying or demeaning, but is not sexual. Bullying is a type of harassment. The growing practice of hazing is also a type of harassment. Harassment of any kind is becoming more commonplace and demands a zero tolerance policy.

16. *In the absence of a court order, a non-custodial parent has no right to information about his or her child.* **FALSE.**

A parent who loses custody of a child is still a parent with certain rights. Those rights include the ability to review school records and to receive unofficial copies of them, as well as to discuss the child and his or her progress with school officials. The question of whether those rights extend to religious education and other ministerial situations has not been settled by the courts. In the absence of any definitive court ruling, it seems prudent to assume that parental rights will apply in religious education and ministerial settings.

The right of access to the child is not necessarily included in non-custodial parent rights. Administrators must consult the appropriate court documents granting custody to see what the custody arrangement is and whether the non-custodial parent has right of access to the child at specific times. Custody arrangements and their implications will be discussed in greater detail in a later chapter.

17. Copyright law allows ministers and educators to make copies of materials that are used for a "good" purpose. **FALSE.**

For many years, administrators of schools and parish ministers seemed to operate from a belief that if whatever was being copied was being used for an educational or other "good" purpose, there could be no violation of copyright law. Some volunteers may have heard little, if anything, about copyright law and its requirements. Having a good intention does not excuse one from compliance with the requirements of copyright law. Making multiple copies of written materials, music and software as well as copying movies and television programs for use in classes or activities almost always violates the copyright law, particularly if the copying is done to avoid purchasing copies. In the case of television programs, keeping and storing copied materials can violate Congressional Guidelines. Some companies, such as Disney, strictly forbid the use of their videos (even if purchased) for classroom use unless there is a clear educational purpose; thus, showing a Disney film for entertainment is not permitted.

18. It is perfectly acceptable to correspond with young people from an adult's personal or home e-mail address. **FALSE.**

Ten years ago many people were not using e-mail; today most people use it. It is a both a blessing and a curse. It is a blessing in that it allows instant communication with persons all over the world or next door. It is a curse in that one can feel held hostage by the perceived demands of answering e-mail and in the reality that the written word, particularly as quickly typed in e-mail, can be open to misunderstanding and misinterpretation. In the past three years, there have been several cases involving Catholic schoolteachers and parish personnel whose e-mail contacts with young persons were deemed inappropriate by parents and/or others.

Adult educators and ministers can best protect themselves by using their parish or school e-mail accounts and thus giving a professional "look" to e-mails. If no parish or school e-mail account is provided, the adult should consider setting up a separate mailbox to which young persons can send e-mails and from which the adult may send messages. A list of suggestions regarding e-mails will be offered later in the book.

19. Ministers and religious educators should not be afraid to remain alone with young people who seek advice. **TRUE (with caveats).**

In the wake of the sexual abuse allegations and the response made in the *Bishops' Charter on the Protection of Young People*, extreme caution is in order. At least one diocese has a directive that adults are never to be alone with a single young person. While the reasons for such a rule are understandable, the directive may put adults in untenable positions. What is a minister to do when, locking up he or she finds a distraught young person asking for help? There may not even be another adult in the building or in the near vicinity. If the weather is warm, the adult can certainly go outside with the young person. Of course, the weather may not always be warm.

The best rule of thumb may well be, "Never stay alone in a room with a young person unless the door is open or there is a window through which others can easily see into the room." This topic and the larger topic of avoiding the appearance of impropriety will be discussed in greater detail later.

20. What one may legally do may not be the most moral or ethical action to take. **TRUE.**

Many times religious educators, youth/campus ministers, and others have asked the question, "Can I legally do this?" when contemplating some particular action. Often, the questioner wants a simple yes or no answer, while the reality is usually a bit more complex. Just because one can legally do something does not mean it is the "right" thing to do. A youth minister may legally tell a young person that he or she may not come back to the program. But first, questions need to be asked: Why do you want to take this action? Have you talked with the student? Expressed your concerns? Given a chance for improvement? We would do well to remember that each of us will be required to give an accounting of our actions before God. The wise decision-maker will ask: What is the right action to take? Looking at what the law allows and the Gospel demands, what should I do?

The following chapters will offer an overview of the laws impacting religious education and campus/youth ministry in general and give a more in-depth presentation of some of the topics mentioned above.

Chapter Two

Civil Law Affecting Ministry with Young People: What Is It? Where Does It Come From? What Does It Mean for Religious Educators, Youth Ministers and Campus Ministers?

I F MOST PEOPLE WHO MINISTER in religious education, youth ministry and campus ministry were to be asked how knowledge of legal requirements affected their choice of ministry, the answer would probably be "not at all." Twenty-five years ago it would have been rare to find workshops or articles dealing with legal issues in religious education or youth/campus ministry. More recently, however, even before the sexual abuse crisis, most people involved in religious education or ministry have attended workshops or read information discussing the requirements of civil law in religious education and Church ministry. It is a good idea to be knowledgeable about the law and its impact on ministry.

Canon Law

Before beginning a presentation of civil law, it is important to discuss Canon Law or Church law. Canon Law is the body of law developed by the Church to govern the actions and relationships of Church members and officials. Canon Law is a separate area of study and ministers (including lay people) successfully completing the prescribed courses and other requirements can receive either a licentiate or a doctorate in Canon Law. They can serve on marriage tribunals and represent people in the Church's court system. Civil courts do practice the doctrine of judicial restraint; they will not substitute their opinion on religious matters, for example, for those of religious officials. However, Canon Law will not take precedence in a civil court over civil law if the matter before the court involves a civil matter. For example, in 1982 some religious sisters in New Hampshire sued the superintendent and the bishop in the case of *Reardon v. LeMoyne*, when their contracts were not renewed for the following year. The trial court accepted the diocese's argument that it was protected under the First Amendment doctrine of separation of church and state. However, the state supreme court reversed the finding and held that since the sisters signed civil employment contracts, civil law prevailed. Those who work in ministry in the Catholic Church have a responsibility to observe the provisions of Canon Law *and* civil law.

Civil Law

Laws affecting Catholic education and ministry in the United States today can generally be classified in four categories: (1) constitutional law (both state and federal); (2) statutes and regulations; (3) common law principles; and (4) contract law.

Constitutional Law

Religious educators and youth/campus ministers are probably familiar with certain Constitutional rights. The First Amendment guarantees freedom of speech, press, assembly and religion; the Fourth Amendment protects against unlawful searches and seizures; the Fifth and Fourteenth Amendments guarantee due process. Workers in public schools or in any government-sponsored program or entity can, of course, claim constitutional rights because they work in government agencies, and those who administer such agencies are public officials—the actions they take can be presumed to be actions of the state or government. Federal Constitutional law protects individuals from the arbitrary deprivation of their Constitutional freedoms by government and government officials. Persons in private institutions cannot claim Constitutional protections because the Constitution governs what public institutions can do, not what private institutions can do.

The restrictions that can be imposed by private institutions may seem unfair, but upon reflection they are not unusual. If a person goes to work in a supermarket, the person will probably be required to wear a uniform. The employee will not be permitted to wear a button advertising a different supermarket chain.

On the other hand, many actions which are prohibited in public schools are permitted in Catholic schools. For example, the First Amendment to the U.S. Constitution protects the rights of persons to free speech;

hence, administrators in public institutions may not prohibit the expression of an unpopular political viewpoint simply because it is unpopular. A landmark U.S. Supreme Court decision in 1969, *Tinker v. Des Moines Independent School District*, produced the now famous statement, "Students and teachers do not shed their constitutional rights at the [public] schoolhouse gate." Since no such protection exists in the private sector, religious educators and campus/youth ministers *can* restrict the speech of both staff and young people. For example, any discussion supporting a women's right to have an abortion could be forbidden.

The bottom line is that when one enters a private institution such as a parish or school, one voluntarily surrenders the protections of the Constitution. A catechist, minister or student can always leave the school or the parish, but so long as the person remains in the institution, constitutional protections are not available. Thus, religious education and campus/youth ministry programs do not have to accept behaviors about which the public sector has no choice but to accept and even to protect.

The only situation in which a Catholic or other private institution can be required to grant federal Constitutional protections is one in which "state action" can be found to be so pervasive within the institution or program that the institution's contested action can fairly be said to be an action of the state. The key factor in state action is the nexus or relationship between the state and the challenged activity. Although some litigants have alleged state action in Catholic educational programs, no court of record has found state action present in private educational programs. Since religious education and ministry programs are not bound to grant Constitutional protections unless state action is found, those alleging a denial of constitutional due process in them will have to prove the existence of significant state action in the contested activity before a court will grant relief.

In an era of ever increasing litigation, some persons with complaints will threaten lawsuits, even if they have no intention of filing suit. It is not uncommon for parents, students or catechists to claim that their constitutional rights have been violated in a religious education or ministry program when, in fact, no constitutional rights existed in the first place. One way to prevent possible misunderstanding is to develop and disseminate comprehensive handbooks which outline the rights and responsibilities of parents and youth participants/students.

Fairness and Due Process

The United States Supreme Court ruled in 1985 in *New Jersey v. T.L.O.* that public school officials may use a "reasonableness" standard rather than a "probable cause" standard in conducting searches of young people and their possessions. Religious education and campus/youth ministry programs are not bound by this case; however, common sense and Gospel respect for young persons should govern searches in any program sponsored by the Catholic Church.

Public entities must be concerned with Constitutional issues. Private programs, while not bound to grant constitutional freedoms *per se*, are bound to act in a manner characterized by **fairness**. Some legal experts talk about a "smell" test. If an action "smells" wrong when a person examines it, it may be suspect. For example, if a campus or youth minister were to tell a student, "You are dismissed from the program, and I am not giving you a reason," an objective observer would probably find that the action "smells" wrong. People do have rights, even if not grounded in the Constitution, to be treated fairly. Dismissing a student and refusing to give a reason do not seem to constitute fairness. In the end, the actions expected of private programs may appear much like constitutional protections. In no area is this more evident than in due process considerations.

The Fifth Amendment to the Constitution guarantees that the federal government will not deprive someone of "life, liberty or property without due process of law." The Fourteenth Amendment made the Fifth Amendment applicable to the states.

Persons entitled to Constitutional due process have what are called **substantive due process rights**; property interest, that can be the subject of ownership, such as jobs and education; and liberty interests, which can include personal freedom and reputation. Substantive due process involves moral as well as legal ramifications: Is this action fair and reasonable? Substantive due process applies whenever property or liberty interests can be shown to exist in the public sector.

The Constitution also guarantees **procedural due process**, or **how** a deprivation occurs. In the public sector, procedural due process includes **notice**, a presentation of the allegations against the accused; **hearing**, an opportunity to respond **before an impartial tribunal**; opportunity to **confront and and cross-examine accusers**; and the opportunity to **call witnesses in one's own behalf**. In serious cases in the public sector, a person also has the right to **have an attorney present, the right to a transcript of the proceeding and the right to appeal.**

Programs sponsored by the Catholic Church, while not bound to provide the whole panoply of procedural due process protections that public sector programs must provide, are nonetheless expected to be fair. An Ohio court, ruling in a significant Catholic school expulsion case, *Geraci v. St. Xavier High School*, stated that courts could intervene in private sector disciplinary cases, if "the proceedings do not comport with fundamental fairness." Fundamental fairness in a Catholic program is akin to, but not synonymous with, constitutional due process.

Federal and State Statutes

Federal and state statutes and regulations comprise a second source of the law which affects Catholic catechetical and ministerial personnel. So long as what is required does not unfairly infringe upon the rights of the Church and can be shown to have some legitimate purpose, Catholic programs can be compelled to comply with them. Failure to comply with reasonable regulations can result in the imposition of sanctions. The 1983 United States Supreme Court case of *Bob Jones v. United States* illustrates. When Bob Jones University was found to use racially discriminatory admissions and disciplinary policies, the Internal Revenue Service withdrew the university's tax-exempt status based on a 1970 regulation proscribing the granting of tax-exempt status to any institution that discriminated on the basis of race. Before a Catholic institution or program will be forced to comply with a law or regulation, the state must demonstrate a *compelling interest* in the enforcement of the regulations. Black defines compelling interest as a: "Term used to uphold state action in the face of attack, grounded on Equal Protection or First Amendment rights because of serious need for such state action" (p. 256).

In *Bob Jones* the government's compelling interest in racial equality was sufficient for the court to order the university to comply with the anti-discrimination laws or lose its tax-exempt status. The university chose to relinquish the tax-exempt status.

Copyright Law

One example of statutory law that has great, even if not fully appreciated, significance for religious education and campus/youth ministry programs is that of copyright law. It is also probably one of the most often violated—generally, without the offender having any appreciation of the fact that he or she is breaking statutory law.

Most people realize that copyright law exists. If asked, many would respond that there are rules that should be followed when making copies of articles, book chapters, computer programs and television programs. Administrators, catechists, ministers and other staff members have seen notices warning patrons using copy machines that they are subject to the provisions of the copyright law.

For some individuals, the fact that apprehension and prosecution for breaking the copyright law rarely become reality becomes a license to break the law. For others, their motive of helping students and young people learn is an excuse for failing to comply with the law.

One commentator has observed: "Although this act [copying] may appear innocent on the surface, copyright infringement, whether malicious or not, is a criminal act. One's position as a teacher and having only the best interests of your students at heart' does not give anyone the right to copy indiscriminately" (Merickel, "The Educator's Rights to Fair Use of Copyrighted Work.")

Reasons to copy

In the 1960s and 1970s budgetary considerations were the reasons given by Catholics who copied songs from copyrighted works and used the copies to compile parish or school hymnals. Courts have consistently struck down such uses and have ordered the offending churches or schools to pay damages. Today, parishes appear to be aware of the legal consequences of copying. They pay for the licensing arrangements of music companies allowing the institution to make as many copies of music as desired during the span of the contract.

However, some catechists and ministers may still wish to copy such items as whole workbooks, other consumable materials, large portions of books and other print materials. The swift advance of technology has catapulted computer programs, videocassettes, DVDs, CDs and similar media into the sphere of copying.

Upon reflection, most ministers and catechists would agree that copyright protection is a just law. Both the Copyright Act of 1909 (the Old Law) and the Copyright Act of 1976 (the New Law) represent attempts to safeguard the rights of authors. People who create materials are entitled to the fruits of their labors; those who use authors' creations without paying royalties, buying copies or seeking permission are guilty of stealing.

It is tempting to think that copyright infringements and lawsuits are more or less the exclusive domain of large institutions. Certainly, the public learns about large-scale abuses faster than individual abuses. Obviously if a company is going to sue someone, it will seek a person or institution that has been guilty of multiple infringements so that larger damages can be won. It simply doesn't make good economic sense to sue someone who will be ordered to pay only a small amount of damages.

Sometimes, though, lawsuits are brought solely to prove a point. A 1983 case, *Marcus v. Rowley*, involved a dispute between two teachers in the same school. One teacher had prepared and copyrighted a 20-page booklet on cake decorating; the second teacher copied approximately half the pages and included them in her own materials. The amount of money involved was negligible; the author had sold fewer than 100 copies at a price of $2. Nonetheless, the court found the second teacher guilty of copyright violation; her use of the other's materials was not "fair."

What is fair use?

Section 107 of the 1976 Copyright Act deals with "fair use" and specifically states that the fair use of copies in teaching "is not an infringement of copyright."

The "sticking point" is what the term "fair use" means. The section lists four factors to be included in any determination of fair use:

- the purpose and character of the use, including whether such use is of a commercial nature or is for nonprofit educational purposes
- the nature of the copyrighted work
- the amount and substantiality (size)of the portion used in relation to the copyrighted work as a whole
- the effect of the use upon the potential market for or value of the copyright work.

Educators and ministers should have little or no trouble complying with the "purpose and character of the work" factor. Ministers and catechists generally copy materials to aid the educational or faith formation process. It should be noted, however, that recreational use of copied materials such as CDs, DVDs or computer games is generally not allowed under the statute.

"The nature of the copyrighted work" factor can prove a bit more problematic than "character and purpose of the work." Who determines what is the nature of the work—the creator and/or copyright holder, the person making the copies, the judge and/or the jury? Almost any material can be classified as educational in some context; even a cartoon can be found to have some educational purpose if one is willing to look for it. It seems reasonable that, in determining nature, a court would look to the ordinary use of the work and to the author's intent in creating the work.

The "amount and substantiality" of the work copied is especially troublesome in the use of videocassettes, CDs, DVDs and computer programs. Catechists and ministers understand that they are not supposed to copy a whole book, but may not understand that copying a television program or a movie onto videotape or copying a computer program for student use can violate the "amount and substantiality" factor.

In the case of *Encyclopedia Britannica v. Crooks*, an educational company engaged in copying commercially available tapes and television programs for teachers, was found to be in violation of the Copyright Act. The company argued that it was providing an educational service for students and teachers who would otherwise be deprived of important educational opportunities. The court rejected the argument.

Religious educators, ministers and administrators may be tempted to think that their small-scale copying acts could not compare with the scope of the activities in this case. In the majority of instances involving single copying, there is no comparison. The practice of developing libraries of copies has occurred in some religious education and youth ministry programs. Whether the collections are of print materials or non-print materials, such as videotapes, DVDs, CDs and computer programs, the practice of building collections can easily be subjected to the same scrutiny as the *Encyclopedia* case.

The last of the four factors, "effect on the market," is also difficult to apply in the ministerial setting. Arguments can be advanced that young people would not rent or purchase commercially available items, even if the copies weren't available. It appears, though, that use of an author's work without appropriate payment for the privilege, is a form of economic harm. Good faith generally will not operate as an acceptable defense in educational copyright or infringement cases.

The court, in *Roy v. Columbia Broadcasting System*, stated: "The federal copyright statute protects copyrighted works against mere copying, even when done in good faith and even when not done to obtain a competitive advantage over the owners of the copyright in the infringed works" (p. 1151).

Guidelines

A congressional committee developed "Guidelines for Classroom Copying in Not-for-Profit Educational Institutions," printed in *House Report* 94-1476, 94th Congress 2d Sess. (1976). Parish leaders should ensure that staff members have access to copies of the guidelines, which are readily available from local libraries, the Copyright Office, and members of Congress. Although these guidelines do not have the force of law that the statute has, judges have used them in deciding cases. Some examples of the guidelines follow.

For poetry, copying of a complete poem of less than 250 words printed on no more than two pages or of an excerpt of 250 words from a longer poem is allowed. For prose, a complete work of less than 2,500 words or an excerpt from a longer work of not more than 1,000 words or 10% of the work is permissible. The guidelines mandate that copying meet this test of *brevity*.

The copying must be *spontaneous*. The educator must have decided more or less on the spur of the moment to use an item. Spontaneity presumes that a person did not have time to secure permission for use from the copyright holder. A teacher or catechist who decides in September to use certain materials in December has ample time to seek permission. In such a situation, failure to seek permission means that the spontaneity requirement will not be met.

A last requirement is that the copying must not have a *cumulative effect*. Making copies of poems or songs by one author would have a cumulative effect and would mean that collected works of the author would not be bought. Similarly, as indicated above, the practice of "librarying" (building a collection of taped television programs, for example) is not permitted. Copying computer programs is never advisable, unless permission to make copies is included in the purchase or rental agreement.

According to "Congressional Guidelines for Off-Air Recording of Broadcast Programming for Educational Purposes," videotapes (and by extension, CDs) may be kept for 45 days only. During the first 10 days, a teacher or other educator may use the tape once in a class (although there is a provision for one repetition for legitimate instructional review). For the remaining 35 days educators may use the tape for evaluative purposes only.

Pastors, principals, catechetical leaders, youth/campus ministers and board members are responsible for developing policy regarding copyright law and technology; administrators are responsible for supervision of all aspects of the educational process. If a person is charged with copyright violation, it is likely that the administrator will be charged as well. Clear policies and careful monitoring of those policies can lessen exposure to liability. As many legal authorities have observed, copyright violation is stealing. It appears, then, as has been noted by some legal authors that "Thou shalt not steal" remains good law. At the very least, policy should require compliance with copyright laws.

Copyright law does not adequately govern the issues of authorship of materials on the Internet. Some young people (and older ones) believe that if something is on the Internet, it can be used with no attribution given to the author. Some articles have no listed authors. But adults responsible for the education and formation of young persons must teach and insist that everyone observe the rules of honesty and fairness and not claim as their own something they did not write or create.

It may be tempting to believe the oft-quoted line from *The Merchant of Venice,* "To do a great right, do a little wrong." Ethical, moral, and legal imperatives do not accept such rationalization. At the same time, young people have a right to expect that adults will protect them from harm and will exercise vigilance over technological behaviors.

Lastly, educators and other ministers themselves must be models of integrity and observe the laws that grant authors and other creators the right to the fruits of their labors. Obviously, the Internet, television and software were not part of Jesus' lived experience, but it is important to reflect on how He would want us to meet the challenges they present in today's technological, ever-changing world.

The Internet

The television and movie industries police themselves, at least to some extent, but there is no equivalent monitoring system in place in the world of cyberspace. Parents, educators and ministers must maintain constant vigilance. The First Amendment to the Constitution does permit much leeway in terms of expression, but it does not require that children and teenagers be given unlimited access to other persons' self-expression. Even if everyone else in the neighborhood is "surfing the Internet," adults must stand firm and monitor computer usage by the young people for whom they are responsible.

Blogging

Blogging, the practice of keeping diaries on line, raises other areas of concern. Users are supposed to be 18 years old but there is no way to monitor this. Young people are going to these sites and posting their names, addresses, schools and pictures for literally anyone in the world to see. Such publicity makes these young people much easier targets for persons who are seeking to prey on them.

Common Law

The third type of law, which applies to both the public and private sector, is common law, which can be defined as:

> Common law is the general universal law of the land. This law is not derived from STATUTES, but is developed through court decisions over hundreds of years. Common law prevails in England and in the United States and is the controlling law unless abrogated or modified by state or federal statutes. It should be noted that common law may also be abrogated or modified by a constitutional amendment or decision by a higher court which adjudicates a constitutional issue (Gatti and Gatti, p.89).

Common law principles can also be derived from God's law and such precepts as the Golden Rule. Many common law principles may be reflected in basic morality such as that found in the Ten Commandments and in other religious writings.

Prior judicial decisions comprise an important part of common law. These decisions are often referred to as "precedents." When a lawsuit is begun, attorneys on both sides begin searching for precedents, prior cases that will support their arguments. In the United States these prior decisions can be found in courts of record from the beginnings of this country. The United States system of common law also embraces all English cases prior to the establishment of the United States. It is not unusual to find old English cases cited in modern cases.

Contract Law

The fourth type of law governing both the public and private sector is contract law. For example, public schools are governed by contract law in some instances, especially in the area of teacher contracts. Courts can construe staff handbooks as contracts in the private sector. However, most cases involving public sector contracts also allege violation of Constitutionally protected interests as well, so contract law is not the only applicable law.

Most cases involving Catholic parishes and schools allege contract violations. The remedy for breach of contract is damages, not reinstatement. Breach of contract can be defined as occurring "when a party does not perform that which he or she was under an absolute duty to perform and the circumstances are such that his or her failure was neither justified nor excused" (Gatti and Gatti, p. 124).

In Catholic parishes and programs, contract law is the predominant governing law. A contract may be defined as: "An agreement between two or more persons which creates an obligation to do or not to do a particular thing" (Black, pp. 291-92.) Generally, the five basic elements of a contract are considered to be: (1) mutual assent (2) by legally competent parties for (3) consideration (4) to subject matter that is legal and (5) in a form of agreement which is legal.

Mutual assent implies that two parties entering into a contract agree to its provisions. A catechetical leader or campus/youth minister agrees to provide services and, in return, the parish or program accepts that offer and pays a salary. Traditional contract law teaches that a contract will only be considered a true instrument if there has been both an offer by the first party and an acceptance of the same by the second party.

Consideration is what the first party agrees to do for the other party in exchange for something from the second party. For example, a parish hires a youth minister full-time and the youth minister agrees to work at least 35 hours a week. Each party to a contract receives a *benefit* and each incurs a *detriment* such as time commitment, etc. If there is no mutual "give and take," a contract does not exist.

Legally competent parties means that the parties entering into the contract are lawfully qualified to enter into the agreement. *Legal subject matter* assumes that the provisions of the contract are legal. *Legal form* may vary from state to state.

The old, but still very relevant, 1973 case, *Weithoff v. St. Veronica's School* is an example of breach of contract. A teacher was dismissed for marrying a priest who had not been laicized and she incurred the Canon Law penalty, which was Church practice at the time, of excommunication from the Church. The teacher had signed a contract binding her to the "promulgated policies" of the parish. The parish school board had enacted a policy requiring all teachers to be practicing Catholics; the policy, however, was kept in the secretary's files and never promulgated to the teachers. The court found for the teacher because the school did not meet its obligation of promulgation.

In a more recent case, *Little v. St. Mary Magdalene*, the court ruled that a non-Catholic teacher in a Catholic school who had signed an agreement containing a "cardinal's clause" requiring her to live a life consistent with the teachings of the Catholic Church had violated that agreement when she married a divorced Catholic who had not yet received an annulment, even though such a marriage was perfectly acceptable in the teacher's religion.

Little and *Weithoff* illustrate that the courts will look to the provisions of contracts in breach of contract cases and will base decisions on what the parties involved have agreed to do, and not on what they should have agreed to do or on any other factor. Courts have upheld the right of private institutions, particularly those sponsored by a Church or religious group, to make rules of conduct that would not be permitted in public institutions. However, the private institution should have policies that prohibit certain types of conduct before it can dismiss a teacher for misconduct.

The case of *Holy Name School of the Congregation of the Holy Name of Jesus of Kimberly v. Dept. of Industry, Labor and Human Relations, and Mary P. Retlick* illustrates. Retlick's contract was not renewed because she married a divorced Catholic man who had not obtained an annulment of his first marriage. The school sought to prove that she was not entitled to unemployment benefits because she willfully violated her contract. Retlick, however, was able to demonstrate that the only policy the school had regarding divorced and remarried teachers concerned religion teachers. Further, the principal had encouraged the teacher to live with the man rather than marry him if she could not marry within the Church, so the school's defense that the marriage was immoral could not withstand judicial scrutiny. Retlick received unemployment.

Courts will consider the characteristics and behavior of the parties involved in a contract. Just as the principal's behavior in *Holy Names* discredited the allegation of immoral behavior in the teacher's action, in a different case a teacher's behavior led the court to find that the teacher should have known that his conduct did not meet the norms of the sponsoring school. In the Louisiana case, *Bischoff v. Brothers of the Sacred Heart*, a former Catholic seminarian, who had been twice divorced and remarried without the appropriate annulments, was held to have been responsible for knowing what the school required. Once the school learned of his marriages, the school rescinded its contract, and Mr. Bischoff sued. The court ruled, "Plaintiff testified he was aware of Catholic dogma regarding divorce and we conclude, as did the Trial Jury, that the plaintiff's bad faith caused error and the contract was void *ab initio*" (p. 151).

The First Amendment guarantee of separation of church and state is not a license for a Church-sponsored institution to do anything its administrators wish. The *Holy Names* case illustrates that, while courts will not rule on the rightness or wrongness of a given religious doctrine, they will look to see whether the action based on the doctrine is reasonable and consistent. The *Weithoff* case illustrates the need for clear polices that are disseminated to all. These cases helped to establish the fact that persons in the private sector do have rights that will be protected by the courts. Administrators are required to know what those rights are and to provide protection.

The *Little* case demonstrates that Catholic schools have the right to hold people to behavioral regulations based on religion, even if an individual's personal religious beliefs would permit the behavior. Legally sound written policies and guidelines greatly facilitate both the knowledge and protection of the rights of all.

Recent Student Discipline Case Alleging Breach of Contract

A July 15, 2004 opinion from the Rhode Island Supreme Court, *Russell Gorman, Jr. et al. v. St. Raphael Academy*, a case alleging breach of contract in a student discipline dispute, represents a victory for all Catholic schools and programs. The decision clearly supports the right of Catholic schools and programs to establish reasonable rules and regulations. The *Gorman* court ruled that courts have no right to interfere in private school disciplinary regulations unless they violate law or public policy. Because this case is recent and pivotal, a comprehensive discussion follows.

The Facts

Russell Gorman, Jr. entered St. Raphael Academy in Pawtucket, Rhode Island in the fall of 2001. Russell wore his hair six to eight inches below the shirt collar in the back. Shortly after the beginning of his freshman year, school officials instructed him to cut his hair or face expulsion. Russell, with his parents' support, refused. The parents sought and were granted a temporary restraining order keeping the school from expelling Russell for his hair length.

The principal revised the school handbook for the 2002–2003 school year to include a new hair-length regulation stipulating that the hair of male students could be no longer than the bottom of the shirt collar. School officials testified that Russell's parents were notified of the impending rule change before the end of the school year; the parents claimed that they did not know of the change until the summer and were not given a new handbook until August of that year when they filed an amended complaint alleging breach of contract and seeking injunctive relief.

The legal arguments and decisions

The trial judge, relying on a public school case, held that the rule was arbitrary and capricious and that the school's rules had to be related to the mission of the school. In effect, the judge violated the principle of judicial restraint which holds that courts do not generally substitute their opinions for those of the professionals. St. Raphael appealed the decision, which could have had the effect of eventually making every Catholic school, parish and program rule subject to judicial scrutiny.

The Gormans alleged breach of contract; St. Raphael argued that the Gormans did not identify the alleged contract, its terms or breach. St. Raphael further argued that the judge improperly placed the burden of proof on the school.

The state supreme court found that the trial judge applied equitable, rather than legal contract principles, to the claim. An equitable remedy is only available when there is no adequate remedy at law. The long-standing general principle has been that the remedy for breach of a contract for personal services (e.g. private education) is damages, not reinstatement, because courts will not compel performance of such a contract if one of the parties does not wish to perform. Additionally, the school argued that since the parents did not sign the 2002–2003 contract in the school handbook, no valid contract could exist.

The trial judge suggested that the Gormans had a four-year contract for Russell's education, a suggestion that the state supreme court rejected while it held that the contract was an annual one subject to renewal.

Question of First Impression

The state supreme court opinion held that this decision was one of first impression, the first time such a conflict had been litigated. Further, the justices observed that they could find no published case in any jurisdiction that dealt with hair-length rules in private educational institutions. Thus, this decision is groundbreaking.

Contract Law Rulings

The court stated, "Because contracts for private education have unique qualities, we must construe them in a manner that leaves the school administration broad discretion to meet its educational and doctrinal responsibilities." Handbooks can be considered contracts. Parents of St. Raphael's students are required to sign tuition contracts agreeing to the terms of the student handbook. Therefore, the court held that the relationship between students/parents and the school has to be a contractual one. The court held that, "... absent a violation of law or public policy, it is not within the province of the court to inject itself in the rule-making authority of a private school."

The court recognized that some public school litigants have alleged that the right to wear one's hair the way one wishes is a Constitutional freedom guaranteed by the First Amendment but, following earlier federal decisions, held that a private school would have to be a state actor before it would be required to recognize constitutional rights. Therefore, no Constitutional protections exist.

Catholic schools and parish programs everywhere owe a debt of gratitude to St. Raphael's Academy. The willingness of the school and the diocese to fight for the right of Catholic institutions to enact and enforce rules makes administration an easier task and underscores the reality that contract law, not constitutional law, governs Catholic schools, parishes and programs. One could legitimately expect a similar verdict in a case involving religious education or campus/youth ministry.

Legal History: How does it Impact Current Case Developments?

An understanding of the historical basis for private sector legal decisions is essential for directors of religious education, campus and youth ministry. Today's "big" issues, while different in some ways from those of past decades, are much the same in others. A brief discussion of the most current "hot" topics will be offered in subsequent chapters.

The third millennium holds new legal challenges for all in the ministry of religious education. Law is not ministry, but it is a boundary around ministry. Moving outside the legal boundary can cause legal problems. The law is, at its core, based on common sense, although it must be frankly admitted that this basis is not always readily apparent. The following chapters will attempt to discuss the common sense implications of current legal issues facing religious education and campus/youth ministry.

Chapter Three

Tort Law: Issues of Liability

THE PREVIOUS CHAPTER discussed the sources of the law affecting ministry and religious education in the United States. This chapter will discuss tort law, including negligence. Tort cases, some of the most common types of legal action brought under statutory and regulatory law, are the ones most frequently brought against educators and ministers. Knowledge of torts and the kinds of cases that can arise should provide the preventive knowledge needed to "stay out of court."

A tort, according to Black, is "a private or civil wrong or injury ... for which the court will provide a remedy in the form of an action for damages" (p. 1489). Historically, torts are generally classified in education law in four categories: **corporal punishment , search and seizure, defamation and negligence**. Many of the relatively new causes of action being brought in such areas as confidentiality, boundaries, harassment and related issues are negligence cases. Since negligence is the most often litigated tort, it will be considered last in this chapter. It should be noted that the law governing torts is virtually the same in both the public and private sectors.

Abuse

As events of the recent past indicate, one of the most serious issues confronting the Catholic Church is child abuse. Abused young persons often choose catechists, campus ministers, youth ministers or other staff as confidants. Therefore, all employees and volunteers should be as prepared as possible to deal with the realities of abuse and neglect. All of the fifty states have statutes governing the reporting of child abuse. Some states have long lists of mandated reporters. Some simply require any and all adults to report. Regardless of whether one is mandated to report, religious educators, catechists, and those who work in campus and youth ministry should not hesitate to make a report to authorities if they have a reasonable suspicion that children or adolescents are being abused in any way. Further, parish policies should require that staff spend some time reviewing pertinent state law and parish/school/program policies and providing information and discussion on the topic at one of the first staff meetings of the year. If a separate meeting is not provided for other employees and volunteers, parish leaders should consider having them present for the appropriate portion of the staff meeting.

Statutory considerations

Compliance with these reporting statutes may not be as easy as it first appears. What arouses suspicion in one adult may not in another. Some statutes mention "reasonable suspicion." These standards could result in two adults viewing the same situation and reaching completely different conclusions. In such cases, courts have to determine whether each individual sincerely believed in the correctness of his or her perception. Despite the best of intentions and efforts, staff members may fail to report suspected child abuse. In that case, the pastor and/or the administrator can be held liable for failure to report under the doctrine of *respondeat superior*, "let the superior answer." However, if an appropriate policy is in place and has been properly implemented, responsibility for failure to report should be that of the individual staff member who failed, not of the institution or supervisor.

Statutes generally mandate reporting procedures. The reporting individual usually makes a phone report that is followed by a written report within a specified time period, often 48 hours, although some states do have different procedures.

Statutes usually provide protection for a person who makes a good-faith report of child abuse that later is discovered to be unfounded. Such a good-faith reporter will not be liable to the alleged abuser for defamation of character. However, a person can be held liable for making what is referred to as a "malicious report," one which has no basis in fact and which was made by a person who knows that no factual basis existed. Conversely, statutes usually mandate that a person who knew of child abuse or neglect and failed to report it can be fined and/or charged with a misdemeanor or felony.

Defining Abuse

What is child abuse? An attorney once defined it as "corporal punishment gone too far." Although it excludes sexual abuse, the definition has merit. However, it poses questions: How far is too far? Who makes the final determination? Can what one person considers abuse be considered valid parental discipline by another? Are there any allowances for differing cultural practices? It is difficult to give a precise definition that will cover all eventualities. Certainly, some situations are so extreme that there can be little argument that abuse has occurred.

Many law enforcement officials and some attorneys instruct parish leaders and ministers to report everything that young people tell them that could possibly constitute abuse or negligence. They further caution catechists, campus ministers and youth ministers that it is not their job to determine if abuse has occurred. In today's climate and for the protection of all, this advice should be heeded. If a mandated reporter, an individual has a responsibility to present the information to the agency designated to receive reports. Appropriate officials will then determine whether the report should be investigated further or simply "screened out" as a well-intentioned report that does not appear to be in the category of abuse.

Most states clearly require the person with the suspicion to file the report. The catechist or minister must personally report abuse to the appropriate agency and he or she should notify the supervisor or pastor. Policy and procedure must support state law.

Physical abuse such as corporal punishment is less of an issue today than it was in 1977 when, in *Ingraham v. Wright*, the U.S. Supreme Court ruled that students in public schools do not have the protection of the Eighth Amendment when subjected to corporal punishment, even if the punishment can be considered "cruel and unusual." In 1984 very few states outlawed corporal punishment in schools; today the majority of states forbids its use. New areas of concern have surfaced in more recent times. The concept of corporal punishment has been enlarged to include any bodily touching that can be construed as punitive. Although catechists, campus and youth ministers should know not to hit, shove or even "horse play" with young people, situations can get out of control. Catechetical leaders and other supervisors must remember, and help those they supervise remember, that as adults they must set good examples and not allow physically harmful behavior.

Emotional Abuse

Mental or emotional abuse is another reportable type of abuse. Claims of mental abuse do not seem to have received serious consideration in the 70's and 80's; today, it is not uncommon for teachers and other supervising adults to be accused of mental abuse or for staff to hear reports of mental abuse from their students. How then is a catechist or minister to know what to report?

Who Should File the Report?

In the past it was not unusual to have a policy requiring that the administrator or supervisor make all child abuse and/or neglect reports, so that the same person was reporting all situations in a given program. This approach, if taken today, can be extremely problematic as states clearly require the person with the suspicion (the religious educator, minister or volunteer) to file the report. Certainly, the administrator can be present when a staff person or volunteer makes a report.

Administrators should decide in advance how visits and requests from police or social workers will be handled. States now require that school personnel allow officials to examine and question students. Administrators, counselors or ministers may request to remain with the student while he or she meets with police or social workers, but the investigating official has the right to refuse to allow personnel to be present.

How Can A Parish/School Protect Young People?

It is a well-established reality that schools and churches can attract persons with abusive tendencies who are seeking children upon whom to prey. Thus, parish and school leaders must do everything in their power to investigate the background of persons before they begin employment or volunteer activities.

Any complaint by a young person or parent alleging child abuse by a catechist, campus minister, youth minister or other staff member, whether paid or volunteer, must receive serious attention. Failure to do so can put the institution and its officials at grave legal risk. Administrators should adopt policies governing reporting child abuse/neglect by staff *before* the need for such policies surfaces. It is preferable to have a policy that is never needed than to have no policy and be forced to try to construct one when faced with a need.

Harassment and Bullying

In the midst of today's litigation involving the Church, those involved in ministry to young persons find their legal "antennae" more attuned than ever to potential problem areas. Two such areas of concern are harassment and bullying. While persons are generally aware of issues surrounding sexual harassment, issues related to non-sexual harassment, including bullying, are less clear.

One may well ask, "What exactly is harassment? We talk about it a great deal, but I've yet to see a good, general definition." The ultimate legal authority for definitions is *Black's Law Dictionary* which defines harassment as:

> Used in variety of legal contexts to describe words, gestures and actions which tend to annoy, alarm and abuse (verbally) another person. A person commits a petty misdemeanor if, with purpose to harass another, he: (1) makes a telephone call without purpose of legitimate communication; or (2) insults, taunts or challenges another in a manner likely to promote a disorderly response; or (3) makes repeated communications anonymously or at extremely inconvenient hours, or in offensively coarse language; or (4) subjects another to an offensive touching; or (5) engages in any other course of alarming conduct serving no legitimate purpose of the actor.

Harassment occurs, then, when one person makes repeated verbal or physical contacts with another person who does not want these contacts. Sexual harassment is a particular type of harassment that involves sexual comments, innuendo, invitations and/or requests for sexual favors. Sexual harassment, which will be discussed in the next section, is generally fairly clear; other types of harassment can be more blurred and may be harder to identify.

Bullying is a type of harassment that involves some sort of force, whether overt or subtle. For example, today exclusion is widely considered to be a form of bullying, even though there may be no apparent contact. By ignoring and/or excluding an individual from participation, the bully shows his or her power.

The real problem in harassment cases is a failure to respect the dignity of another. Since there are many ways to exhibit disrespect, administrators would be well advised to consider having a rule that simply forbids all demeaning behavior. There is a place, of course, for more detailed listings of possible offenses, but more general catch-all clauses ensure that most inappropriate behaviors can be "caught" and persons held accountable under the more general provision.

Under the previously-cited doctrine of *respondeat superior*, let the superior answer, supervising adults can be held liable for one young person's harassment or bullying of another. If an adult knows or has been informed that one student is harassing another and fails to act, he or she can be held liable for the harassment. Although the majority of such cases involve sexual harassment, the potential for liability for other types of harassment exists as well. Thus, those exhibiting demeaning behaviors must be immediately corrected.

Directors of religious education, catechists, campus ministers, youth ministers and volunteers really have five main duties in these areas which can be placed under the broad, general category of demeaning behavior. They are:

(1) *the duty to minimize risks*: supervisors should periodically examine practices and routines to see if there are times and places when bullying and harassment are more likely to occur and should then make plans to minimize the likelihood of occurrence.

(2) *the duty to educate young people*: adults need to show in word and deed that demeaning behavior is not appropriate.

(3) *the duty to investigate complaints and concerns*: if a young person expresses discomfort, the administrator, catechist, minister or volunteer should carefully investigate the situation while remembering that things may not always be what they seem.

(4) *the duty to remedy violations*: supervisors should swiftly and firmly correct those who engage in demeaning behaviors.

(5) *the duty to monitor students and situations*: those who supervise children and adolescents should remember the old "eyes in the back of the head" image and pay careful attention to those entrusted to their care.

Educators often ask for practical suggestions in meeting legal responsibilities. Knowledge of law and legal phrases is of little use if one cannot put the ethical principles that drive the law into practice. The following are ten suggestions.

Harrassment Prevention and Intervention Techniques

1. Create a climate where all are valued.
2. Observe young people at times when you are not "in charge."
3. Watch for the warning signs of isolation, depression and suppressed anger.
4. Err on the side of caution when expressing concerns about behaviors and attitudes.
5. Do not keep secrets.
6. Tell young people that you will keep confidences only if health, life, safety and/or criminal activity are not at issue.

7. When assigning young persons to groups, use random methods rather than self-selection.
8. Do not allow name-calling or demeaning comments.
9. Listen to what is said as well as to what is not said.
10. Remember that supervision is a *mental* as well as a *physical* act.

Sexual Harassment

Catechetical leaders, youth and campus ministers are right to be concerned about the possible liability of the parish if one young person alleges sexual harassment by anyone, even another student, while participating in a parish activity. What exactly is sexual harassment and how should it be handled?

Virtually everyone recognizes the term, "sexual harassment." Providing a working definition and appropriate policies and procedures, however, is not easy. No longer is sexual harassment something that is found only between two adults or between an adult and a child. Children and adolescents can claim that peers have harassed them. What, then, is a catechist or minister to do?

Parish leaders, religious education boards, pastors and other ministers should enact and implement policies prohibiting sexual harassment; federal and state law can assist with this process. Title VII of the Civil Rights Act of 1964 mandated that the workplace be free of harassment based on sex. Title IX requires that educational programs receiving federal funding be free of sexual harassment. Both these titled laws are anti-discrimination statutes. Some *states* are now prohibiting discrimination based on gender; such a requirement would prohibit such statements as, "Boys are better at math than are girls."

Federal anti-discrimination law can bind Catholic institutions. Most schools and parishes routinely file statements of compliance with discrimination laws with appropriate local, state and national authorities. Anti-discrimination legislation can impact Catholic institutions because the government has a compelling interest in the equal treatment of all citizens. Compliance with statutory law can be required if there is no less burdensome way to meet the requirements of the law. Sexual harassment is one type of discrimination.

The Equal Employment Opportunities Commission has issued guidelines that define sexual harassment, forbidden by Title VII, as: "unwelcome sexual advances, requests for sexual favors, and other verbal or physical conduct of a sexual nature" under certain conditions. Specifically, Title IX states: "No person in the United States shall, on the basis of sex, be excluded from participation in, be denied the benefits of, or be subjected to discrimination under any education program or activity receiving federal financial assistance." While the amount of financial assistance necessary to trigger protection has not been established, most Catholic schools, for example, have accepted some government funds or services at some time and thus would be well advised to comply with Title IX as far as possible. Courts, including the U.S. Supreme Court, are vigorously supporting persons' rights to be free from sexual harassment.

A catechist, campus minister or youth minister may ask, "I can see how Catholic schools should be worried about sexual harassment laws because of receipt of government funds for library resources and cafeteria food, but why should religious education and youth programs be worried? We don't take federal money. We don't even qualify for it."

Case law developed over the last twenty years holds that public policy demands the equal treatment of all. For example, Bob Jones University lost its tax-exempt status because it discriminated against people on the basis of race; the university claimed this action was based on sincerely held religious belief. While affirming the right of the institution to practice its religion, the U.S. Supreme Court required that the government provide no assistance to such a discriminatory body; hence, its tax-exempt status was revoked. No Catholic parish or program should ever practice racial or sexual discrimination.

In the 1992 case of *Franklin v. Gwinnet County Public School*, the United States Supreme Court ruled that monetary damages can be awarded students whose rights under Title IX have been violated. In this case a teacher had allegedly sexually harassed a student for several years. The harassment consisted of conversations, kissing, telephone calls and forced sexual relations. The school system maintained that no relief could be given the student since Title IX remedies had been limited to back pay and employment relief. The court disagreed, held that students who suffer harassment are entitled to damages, and remanded the case to the lower court for a determination of damages. Thus, it would appear that if Title IX applies to the Catholic school or institution (and no case to date has held that it does not), young people may be protected against sexual harassment in much the same manner that employees are protected.

Actions that could constitute sexual harassment

The following are examples of behaviors that could constitute sexual harassment: sexual propositions, off-color jokes, inappropriate physical contact, innuendoes, sexual offers, looks, and gestures. In a number of recent public school cases and religious education cases, female students alleged that male students made sexual statements to them and that school officials, after being informed, declined to take action. One director of religious education found herself in "hot water" when the following occurred. A male student and a female student, both approximately thirteen years of age, approached the pencil sharpener at roughly the same time in the religious education classroom. The boy sharpened his pencil and then blew the shavings onto the chest area of the girl's sweater. He then proceeded to say, "Here, let me help you," as he used his hand to remove the shavings from the sweater. The embarrassed girl went to the director of religious education who told her that "boys will be boys." The girl's parents were outraged and threatened legal action. Ultimately, a resolution was reached outside court; it is easy to imagine, however, how a court might have viewed the situation.

Although one can argue that the person who sexually harasses another should be liable and not the parish, school or program, case law is suggesting that administrators who ignore such behavior or do not take it seriously can be held liable to the offended parties.

Suggested Policies

Policies defining sexual harassment and procedures for dealing with claims of sexual harassment should be clear and understandable to the average person. All parish staff members, both paid and volunteer, must be required to implement the policies.

Dioceses generally have policies and procedures for dealing with sexual harassment as part of their sexual abuse or safe environment policies which have been enacted according to the directives contained in the bishops' *Charter for the Protection of Young People*. Every person involved in ministry in any form in a diocese must follow the diocesan policies. The following is simply one of many possible suggestions of a policy statement based on federal law.

Definition:

Sexual harassment is defined as (1) threatening to impose adverse sanctions on a person, unless favors are given; and/or (2) conduct, containing sexual matter or suggestions, which would be offensive to a reasonable person.

Sexual harassment may include, but is not limited to, the following behaviors:

(1) Verbal conduct such as epithets, derogatory jokes or comments, slurs or unwanted sexual advances, imitations, or comments;

(2) Visual contact such as derogatory and/or sexually-oriented posters, photography, cartoons, drawings, or gestures;

(3) Physical contact such as assault, unwanted touching, blocking normal movements, or interfering with work, study, or play because of gender;

(4) Threats and demands to submit to sexual requests as a condition of continued employment or grades or other benefits or to avoid some other loss and offers of benefits in return for sexual favors; and

(5) Retaliation for having reported or threatened to report sexual harassment.

Procedures for reporting should then be given. These procedures should include a statement such as, "All allegations will be taken seriously and promptly investigated." Administrators should stress confidentiality and express concern for both the alleged victim and the alleged perpetrator. Procedures should include copies of the forms used in such cases.

Every parish employee and volunteer should be required to sign a statement that he or she has been given a copy of the policies relating to sexual harassment and other sexual misconduct, has read the material, and agrees to be bound by it. Parent/student handbooks should contain at least a general statement that sexual harassment is not condoned in a Christian atmosphere, and both parents and students should sign a statement that they agree to be governed by the handbook.

Prevention

It is far easier to prevent claims of sexual harassment than it is to defend them. To that end, catechists, ministers and volunteers should participate in some kind of in-service training that raises awareness of sexual harassment and other gender issues. Staff members must understand what sorts of behaviors can be construed as sexual harassment.

Catechists and other ministers should discuss issues of fair treatment with young people, and should promptly correct individuals who demean others. Defenses such as, "I was only kidding," will not be accepted if the alleged victim states that the behavior was offensive and unwelcome, and a court finds that a reasonable person could find the behavior offensive and unwelcome.

Finally, of course, sexual harassment and other forms of demeaning behavior have no place in Catholic parishes and schools. Guarding the dignity of each member of the parish community should be a priority for all involved in the ministries of the Catholic Church.

Privacy Issues

Privacy may seem to be a somewhat elusive concept in these troubled times. Since the World Trade Center tragedy (9/11), the government has taken steps, whether citizens agree with them or not, to provide greater protection from terrorist attacks; some involve actions that previously would have been considered an invasion of privacy. The right to privacy basically means, according to *Black's Law Dictionary*: "The right to be let [sic—left] alone, the right of a person to be free from unwarranted publicity; and the right to live without unwarranted interference by the public in matters with which the public is not generally concerned." The recent HIPAA laws protecting the privacy of persons' medical records is one government action to protect individuals' personal information from being made available to others without the permission of the individual involved.

In terms of schools, the relevant privacy protection can be found in the Buckley Amendment (Family Educational Records Privacy Act) enacted in 1975 which ended the practice of parents being denied access to the official school records of their children. Although whether this Act applies to private schools has never been tested in the United States Supreme Court, the vast majority of dioceses voluntarily comply with its provisions. Administrators, directors of religious education and ministers may wish to do the same. Basically, compliance would mean that any records pertaining to a young person enrolled or participating in a parish or school program would not be shared with anyone except those with a "need to know" and/or with parental permission. Granted, religious education and campus/youth ministry records will probably not contain the kinds of materials that may be problematic in school records, but good practice seems to require protection of students' privacy. Administrators and directors should avoid the practice of having only one file for each student or participant. If a child or adolescent writes a letter alleging abuse or stating fear of a parent or a threat to harm self or others, a staff member should immediately bring that letter to the supervisor who will take or direct appropriate action. The letter or a copy of it should be kept in a separate file. There is no need to keep everything concerning a student/participant in one file and there is a responsibility to protect the reputation of those entrusted to the parish or program.

Defamation of Character

Defamation is the violation of a person's liberty, interest or right to reputation. Defamation is the utterance of words in spoken or written form that are detrimental to the subject's reputation. Defamation can encompass a wide range of remarks; almost anything negative said about someone could be construed as defamatory since it could affect a person's reputation or the esteem in which others hold the person.

The potential for defamation to be alleged certainly exists in parish leaders' relationships with young people and staff. Administrators should be factual in their comments, whether written or oral, about the conduct of others. The news media report defamation cases in which the defendant asserts an affirmative defense of truth. Those who work with young people are often held to a higher standard than are other persons because they hold positions of trust; thus, damage to reputation, rather than truth of the allegation, can determine the outcome.

Privacy and reputation are two serious legal issues facing religious educators and ministers today. Both young people and staff members expect that information concerning them will be revealed only to those with a right to know. Policies should require the use of reasonable measures to safeguard private information.

Defamation, then, is an unprivileged communication that harms the reputation of another. Defamation, which may involve invasion of privacy, can be either spoken (*slander*), or written (*libel*). All members of the faith community should be concerned with protecting the reputations of all. Administrators, catechists and ministers should exercise great care in keeping records, as well as in speaking about behavior. It is only just fair that people involved as leaders in parish ministry refrain from gossip or unnecessary derogatory remarks about members of the parish community.

Search and Seizure

The right to be free from unreasonable, warrant-less searches is guaranteed by the Fourth Amendment to the Constitution. Although Catholic institutions and programs are not bound by the Constitution, it is helpful, when considering the development of policies and procedures, to look at public sector issues. Search and seizure problems occur when a student or participant alleges injury from a search of person or property. Early

45

cases delineated differences between *probable* and *reasonable cause*. Probable cause is a stricter standard than reasonable cause and is held to exist when an official has reliable knowledge about the whereabouts of dangerous or potentially dangerous material on parish grounds, for example. Reasonable cause is a suspicion with some basis in fact. A phone call, a note, or a suspicious appearance can comprise reasonable cause.

Historically, case law indicated that once a public school administrator involves the police in a search or turns seized items over to the police, Fourth Amendment protections apply and improperly seized evidence can be excluded from a trial if criminal convictions are later sought. Thus, an improper search could be a violation of a student's constitutional rights and administrators can be held liable for damages as perpetrators of constitutional torts. However, a rationale for holding public school administrators to a less strict standard than other public officials in search and seizure situations was primarily based on the *in loco parentis* doctrine, which held that school officials have the right to act as a reasonable parent could if he or she suspected a child to be in possession of some illegal or dangerous substance.

Catholic educators and ministers could be subject to private tort suits, such as invasion of privacy or negligent infliction of emotional distress if a young person claims to have been harmed by a search. The search's level of intrusion determines the court's degree of scrutiny. Asking a student to empty his pockets would require a less strict degree of scrutiny than would a body search.

If You Have to Search, How Should You Do It?

Many educators are reviewing the need for policies and procedures regarding student searches. In 1985 the U.S. Supreme Court ruled in *New Jersey v. T.L.O.* that public school administrators did not need search warrants or probable cause (only reasonable cause) to search students and their belongings. The Catholic educator, obviously, is not bound to Fourth Amendment search and seizure requirements. However, as indicated above, schools could be subject to suits for damages if a student alleges harm as a result of an unreasonable search. Common sense precautions are in order. Catechists and other staff members should be given guidelines for any search of a student or his or her belongings. Procedures for searching students should be more stringent than those for searching mere possessions. Strip searches should never be permitted.

Parish property does not belong to the student. Parishes and programs strengthen their legal positions by including a policy in the parent/student handbook that states, "The parish or school is co-tenant of lockers and desks and reserves the right to search them at any time without notice."

Some suggested guidelines for search and seizure protocols follow.

General Considerations Before Search and Seizure

1. Ask yourself if what you are looking for is worth the search. Looking for a lost dollar bill is generally not worth the effort beyond a general question, "Has anyone seen Tommy's dollar?"
2. Ask everyone to search around desks/lockers/in personal items. Approach is everything. A catechist might say, "Let's all look in our pockets and see if Tom's toy might have fallen in"(as the catechist looks in his or her pockets). A youth minister might state, "Mary has lost her ring. Does anyone have any idea where it might be? Could you look in your belongings to see if it may have ended up with your things by mistake?" Have another staff member present in any searches of individual students or property.

Searching Lockers, Desks

1. Ask the child or adolescent if there is anything he or she wishes to show you.
2. Ask the young person to remove the items from the desk and open anything that you direct him or her to open.
3. Put any contraband in a separate container (if it will fit). Have the young person sign a statement that the items were found in the locker or desk. Take the item to the administrator who can "take over," talk with the individual and contact parents, if necessary.
4. If there is nothing illegal or forbidden in the desk or locker, thank the person for cooperating and state that you are glad that the matter has been resolved (in age appropriate language, of course).

Searching Young People and Purses/Coats/Book bags (which can be considered extensions of the person)

1. Ask the individual if you may search his pockets, coat, book bag or purse.
2. If the answer is yes, ask him to take everything out and show it to you.
3. If the answer is no, isolate the individual and the purse or bag under an adult's supervision.

4. Call the parent, explain the situation, tell the parent you would like to clear his or her child's name and ask the parent to either tell the young person to cooperate or to come to the parish or school and conduct the search himself or herself. If the parent refuses, tell the parent that the parish/school-parental partnership appears to be broken and needs immediate attention. Of course, the administrator needs to seek the approval of the pastor or other supervisor before making a statement such as "your child is dismissed from this program."

If the police ask to search a young person:
1. Ask for the officer's identification.
2. Ask if the officer has a warrant. If he or she has one, let the officer proceed. If there is no warrant, politely tell the officer that once one is obtained and presented, you will make the individual available for a search. Notify parents immediately in either scenario. *Exception:* if a clear threat to health or safety is involved, use your best judgment.

Administrators should not hesitate to consult police officers and attorneys when needed. When controversy arises, the best defense is having followed clear policies and procedures.

Community Service Programs

Part of the mission of the Catholic parish is to teach service. The philosophies of most Catholic programs, for example, clearly state that one goal is to develop persons who consider service to others a primary responsibility. To that end, many Catholic have initiated service programs ranging from visiting nursing homes to weekly service opportunities at an off-campus site.

Many parents and young people accept the service component of Catholic programs. Some, however, question the necessity and even the right of the school to insist that all students give service. A few remark that if you are forced to do the service, it isn't service at all, but some form of slavery.

Legal basis

Public schools have also initiated service programs and have received many of the same complaints that Catholic educational administrators have been fielding for years. In 1996, however, the United States Court of Appeals seemed to settle the question of whether service constituted "involuntary servitude" or "slavery." In *Immediato v. Rye Neck School District*, a second circuit New York case, a high school student and his parents brought a civil rights action against the district board of education. The Immediatos alleged that the public school district's mandatory community service program violated their constitutional rights, particularly the 13th Amendment's abolition of slavery, and the 14th Amendment's due process clause. The district court granted summary judgment (judgment without a trial; in determining summary judgment, a court must construe all the facts in the light most favorable to the person who did *not* seek summary judgment) and the parents appealed to the U.S. Court of Appeals.

The public school district's mandatory program required all students to complete 40 hours of community service at some time during their high school years, and to participate in classroom discussion about their service experiences. No exceptions are made for students or parents who object to the service requirement. The program is governed by regulations concerning the types of organizations for which students may perform service, and the nature of the work that is undertaken. The students may not be paid for their work. Twenty hours of the requirement can be satisfied by service to the school, but at least 20 hours must be completed at an off-campus site.

The court found that the community service program and involuntary servitude were not the same thing, and that community service was not prohibited by the 13th Amendment.

The question of the 13th Amendment and involuntary servitude has not been specifically addressed in the private setting. It is obvious that no institution, public or private, will be permitted to practice slavery. However, every action a student is required to take does not constitute involuntary servitude, even if the action is one the student would choose to take.

The findings of the *Immediato* case provide information for the Catholic school or program administrator. Since public schools, which are government agencies charged with protecting the constitutional rights of their students, may have mandatory service programs, schools and parish programs sponsored by the Catholic Church may have them. Catechetical leaders and other ministers may wish to mention the *Immediato* case to questioning parents or students. Clearly, mandatory service programs are lawful.

The Catholic parish can refuse to admit or retain students/participants if they refuse to perform the service that is part of the requirement for successful completion of the program. Sometimes, however, there may be a seemingly good reason for some consideration in the type and location of the service.

For example, a Boston, Massachusetts service program involved serving meals at the Pine Street Inn and at Rosie's Place, both homeless shelters. A few parents said that they felt the area was dangerous and would not permit their daughters to participate. Although adults supervised the students and local buses were rented for transportation, the parents persisted in their statements. Of course, it was the students who were caught in the middle. Ultimately, the students were allowed to perform an alternative service of equal duration at a school-approved site. In this instance, the parents did not object to the *concept* of service, but rather to the *location* of the service.

Parental Notification

The parent/student handbook is a good place to provide initial notification of the existence of a mandatory service program. All program administrators should require that parents sign a statement such as, "We have read and agree to be governed by this handbook," prior to their child's admittance to the program.

In the year or semester in which the service program is held, the administrator or other supervisor should notify the parents of participating students in writing of the requirement, and the notification should reference the previously published statement in the handbook.

Supervision and Liability

It is highly advisable that the catechist, campus minister or youth minister visit all service program sites. Such visits constitute appropriate diligence on the part of the school or parish. Particularly if the service program involves released time from the program or school, the supervisor should make spot checks of sites to ensure that students are in attendance and acting appropriately. If the sheer numbers and times of the service opportunities preclude some checks, the supervisor should be in regular phone contact with the site supervisor to ascertain that young persons are in attendance and that program objectives are being met.

The service program, like all off-campus programs, involves risks. One way to lessen parish and school liability is to ask each site to provide a letter of invitation to the parish or school. In this manner, any liability for injuries occurring on the site should be largely borne by the site. It should be noted, however, that placement sites often require the school or program to indemnify the site from liability for any injury; this requirement means that the parish may have to pay any judgment if the site is sued. If a site requests such an indemnification, the pastor or other administrator should seek appropriate legal counsel.

Off Campus Trips (Field Trips)

Educators have been discussing field trips for years and it may appear that little could be left to say on the subject. Yet there are still issues that need to be revisited. Additionally, new staff and volunteers come "on board" and need education as well. More accidents involving young persons occur in classrooms or other parish meeting places than in all other activities, because such places are where young people spend much of their time. However, off-campus activities are more dangerous than classroom activities simply because of their nature and the hazards involved in transportation. Some attorneys have adopted a "no field trip" position on the theory that if young people aren't taken off-site, they can't get hurt off campus. Most religious educators and campus/youth ministers however, view field trips as an important part of a young person's education. The challenge lies in balancing the risks against the benefits and making an informed, responsible decision.

Educational or Programmatic Purpose

Most attorneys and judges would probably agree that a field trip should have an educational, or, in the case of campus or youth ministry in particular, a programmatic purpose. If an accident were to occur, a parish could much more easily justify an educational trip than one that is purely recreational in nature.

A Michigan school case, *Davis v. Homestead Farms*, illustrates. A horse bit a kindergarten student while she was participating in a field trip to a farm. The court found that the trip to the farm constituted a curricular activity, and suggested a balancing test of risks and benefits. Taking kindergarten children to a farm is definitely educational. While there is some risk involved, parents accepted the risk when they accepted the benefit. In the absence of any evidence indicating that the school failed to provide adequate supervision, the school was held blameless.

Youth ministry programs are allowed more latitude in determining educational or programmatic purposes than are religious education or school programs. Youth ministry generally has goals concerning such issues as socialization and appropriate recreation. However, some reasonable rationale for the trip will be expected.

A cover letter, stating the educational purpose of the trip, should accompany each permission slip. Most dioceses have an attorney-approved permission form included in its policies and procedures. All school, parish and youth/campus ministers should use this form and this form only. At minimum, a parent or guardian should sign a permission form asking that the child/adolescent be allowed to participate in the activity, giving permission for the child's participation and transportation and indemnifying the parish/school and its agents from liability for injury. Additionally, it is advisable to state the educational or programmatic purpose on the form so that there can be no question at a later point. In the unfortunate case in which a student is injured, a parish or school will be in a much better legal position if the educational value of the trip is clearly evident. Parishes and schools may find it very difficult to justify a trip that was taken purely for pleasure.

Liability for Injury

Parents *cannot* sign away their children's rights to safety. Parishes, schools and their employees and volunteers are required to protect the safety of the children entrusted to their care. If a child is injured while participating in a field trip and evidence indicates that the supervising adults failed in their duty to supervise adequately, and if that failure was a significant factor in the student's sustaining an injury, the school/parish and its employees can be held liable for injury. A 2003 public school case, *Maracallo v. B.O.E. of City of New York*, illustrates. Teachers accompanied students on a school trip to a splash park in New York. Believing that the lifeguards were providing supervision, the teachers went to another part of the park. A student drowned. The court found the teachers negligent and stated that supervisory responsibilities cannot be handed off to park employees.

Some people ask, "Why have a permission form if you can be held liable anyway?" While the permission form does not provide absolute protection from all liability for injury, it does provide the best protection available. If an unforeseeable event occurred (a child is hit by a drunk driver or a child is injured when a tool falls from a scaffold), there is a very strong possibility that the parish or school and its employees will be exonerated from blame.

The mythical creature, "the reasonable person," is the standard courts use when considering liability. A court will ask, "Did the adult supervise the young person in a manner that a reasonable person in the same situation could be expected to do? Did a parent sign the permission form?

What exactly did the form say?" The answers to these questions will determine the nature and degree of liability.

Permission Forms

As stated above, educators should use the (Arch)diocesan permission form. If the trip poses special risks such as, for example, proximity to bodies of water, these should be noted either in the cover letter or in an addendum to the form. Indicating the educational or programmatic purpose of the trip is also advisable.

Submitted permission slips should be checked for forgery. The person responsible for the trip should be required to check signatures with those on file on a signature card. Perhaps the school or parish secretary could be given the task of checking all field trip signatures. When one person consistently checks all forms, the likelihood of finding forgeries increases.

A young person who does not have a signed permission form should not be allowed to participate in the outing. A non-standard form such as a handwritten note saying, "Emily can go with you today" should not be accepted, as a parent could always maintain that he or she was not aware of the real destination, educational or programmatic purpose, or risks involved in the trip. If the school or program administrator wishes to fax the form to a parent who will sign and return it, that is permissible.

Transportation to Off-Campus Activities

Many educators have questions about field trips. One of the most often asked questions is, "what kind of transportation must a school provide? Many a person has observed, "If the parish or school cannot afford a bus, it cannot afford the trip." Smaller schools/parishes and/or those with severely limited resources may believe that their students and parents will not be able to pay the additional monies needed for a leased bus. No law requires that buses provide all field trip transportation, but in these days of increasing accidents and litigation, such a law may not be far away. Whatever mode of transportation is chosen, the catechetical leader, campus minister or youth minister must ensure that certain standards are maintained.

The means of transportation should be clearly noted in a cover letter or permission slip. The parents should specifically agree to that means of transportation. If the youth ministry service group rents school buses to provide transportation, and parents have consented to the transportation, participants should not be allowed to use any other transportation unless the parent has clearly given other directions for a specific instance or instances.

If parent drivers are used, the permission slip should contain a clause such as, "We request that our child be allowed to ride in a car driven by a volunteer parent and we give permission. . .." Since relatively few parishes and schools have insurance that covers volunteers driving their own vehicles, it is important for administrators to communicate clearly to parents that their insurance will be primary. Any school or diocesan insurance can be utilized only after the driver's insurance and assets are exhausted. Parents should be required to provide a copy of their proof of insurance that should be kept on file.

Federal and state seat belt laws govern the use of seat belts. No driver should take more children than the number of seat belts in the car. Administrators should give the drivers not only directions to the site, but also rules and procedures for student behavior in cars. Administrators must insist that drivers follow the schedule and not deviate from it, as sometimes happens when a parent decides to buy ice cream cones for those in his car while those in other cars go directly to the site. Case law is well established that such unscheduled trips are not permissible.

At the high school level, it is not uncommon for students to transport themselves and their friends to activities. Often students make their own arrangements. Administrators should ensure that no staff member assigns particular students to a particular driver. In the unfortunate event of an accident or injury, a parent could allege that the supervisor was negligent if the supervisor assigned the student to a particular car. On the way to and from a site, as well as when on the site, high school drivers should not be permitted to take side trips to restaurants, movie houses, etc., unless such activities are part of the planned trip. In one 1982 case involving an overnight camping trip, *Caston v. Buckeye*, a parish was held liable when the priest supervisor allowed a high school boy to drive to a store after everyone had already eaten; the boy was involved in an accident. The court found the side trip unnecessary and ordered the school to pay over a million dollars in damages. Another possible approach is to require parents to provide transportation and to state that the parish accepts no responsibility for that transportation.

Use of Staff Cars

Administrators should clearly understand that no staff person can be required to transport minors in his or her car. Sometimes, school or diocesan insurance will cover employees who transport students on official business; often, it will not. Thus, the administrator needs to check insurance coverage with the carrier or with the agent. In any case, use of staff cars should be discouraged.

Following diocesan/school policies and procedures

Failure to follow diocesan policies and procedures can result in tragedy. In one relatively recent high school case, two athletic coaches failed to follow diocesan policy which required that school-owned or leased buses or vans be used for transport to activities. When one van failed to start, one coach took his own car and had another student drive some students as well. The student was involved in a fatal accident. Certainly, no one wanted anyone to be hurt or killed. If the policy had been followed, however, there probably would have been no tragedy. The case was settled out of court but a family was virtually destroyed and staff members have to live with the reality that their failure to follow policy may have caused a person's death.

Common sense is still a good guideline. Questions such as, "How would I want this handled if my child were participating?" can help administrators, staff and volunteers make good decisions.

Chaperones: What Administrators Need to Know

Few catechists or ministers could imagine offering varied on- and off-site experiences without the services of adult volunteers. Field trips, dances, skating parties, etc., would be severely affected if only certified staff were permitted to serve as chaperones. Increasing litigation demands that chaperones be screened, trained, and supervised for the protection of all. This section will address some of the more common administrative questions.

How Can You Identify Good Volunteer Chaperones?

There is no one foolproof approach to selecting chaperones. Parish leaders must understand one basic fact—everyone who volunteers to chaperone does not have to be accepted for the task. Some persons do not possess the physical or mental competence or the maturity for the job. Others may see chaperoning as a popularity contest and take actions that are not appropriate. Still others may insist on bringing younger children on the trip, or may focus exclusively on their own children.

Parish leaders must be willing to say to a volunteer, "I appreciate your interest, but at this time we cannot use your services." It is not necessary to enter into a prolonged debate about reasons. Simply declining to accept the person as a volunteer is enough.

A person may say, "I understand that I do not have to continue with a volunteer once I know they lack necessary skills. But how can I determine they do not possess the necessary skills before I entrust them with other people's children?" The same methods used to screen other adult volunteers should be employed for chaperones. At the very least, prospective chaperones should have to submit a signed form indicating that they have not been convicted of a crime. There are some situations, however, in which a decades old conviction for a non-violent crime should not be a barrier to volunteering. Some schools and programs now require that all persons volunteering to work with students be fingerprinted or submit to a criminal offenders' record check. In the sad event that a chaperone's action or inaction injures a young person, the program that has a clear screening procedure will be in a much better position than one that does not.

Can Adult Volunteers Chaperone Young People Without a Staff Member Present?

The answer to this question is a resounding yes. There are a few states that require certified personnel to supervise playgrounds; it is commonly accepted, however, that a teacher cannot be everywhere paying attention to everything and supervising the students and chaperones at all times. The same principle would apply to adults who are reasonably performing the duties assigned to them. Courts expect that adult chaperones are reasonably prudent people who have been trained in the duties of their position and who can be expected to perform those duties.

What Kind of Training Should Chaperones Receive?

All volunteers should receive some sort of orientation, even if that orientation takes place fifteen minutes before a field trip departure. Each volunteer should be given a written description of chaperoning duties, school or program rules and consequences. Chaperones must agree to enforce the rules. If for some reason a person ignores the rules, that person should not be allowed to chaperone again.

What Kinds of Problems with Adult Chaperones are Common?

One of the most common problems is administrative failure to orient or explain what is expected of the chaperone. For example, at a high school dance, the principal was amazed to find all the adult chaperones sitting and drinking coffee in the faculty room while two teachers frantically trying to keep order in a noisy gymnasium. When the principal asked the adults why they weren't on the dance floor, she was told that no one had told them to do anything. Such an occurrence is more common than might be thought. Administrators cannot afford to assume that chaperones just "know" what to do.

A second problem can also arise. Volunteer parent-chaperones may appear with younger children and announce that they are coming too since the parent cannot leave them home alone. In such instances, administrators should thank the parents for their interest but explain that they will be unable to serve as chaperones since their attention will necessarily be on their own children, not on the ones assigned to their supervision.

As mentioned earlier, the parent who drives to a field trip and makes unauthorized stops such as at a fast food restaurant or ice cream shop to treat the students presents a third problem. Should accidents or injuries occur, it will be difficult to avoid liability if the situation could have been avoided by following the rules in the first place.

Chaperones are an important part of the total educational experience. Administrators must be sure that: (1) chaperones are properly screened; (2) chaperones receive some sort of orientation and written instructions; and (3) persons who are unable or unwilling to follow school rules and procedures are not allowed to volunteer.

Transportation

Transportation is another problematic area. The means of transportation should be clearly noted in the cover letter or the permission slip for the field trip, unless only one mode of transportation is ever used and that fact is noted in the parent/student handbook. As far as possible, buses should be used for field trips. If parent drivers are used, the permission slip should contain a clause in which the parent agrees to this mode of transportation. If the parish or school does not have insurance covering volunteer drivers, parent drivers should be so notified, should be required to place a copy of their proof of auto insurance on file, and should be told that they can be held liable in the event of accident or injury. The same cautions apply when teachers drive their own cars to transport students. Thus, the use of teacher cars should be discouraged. Administrators should consult their insurance agents or the appropriate archdiocesan officials in this matter.

Overnight Trips

Both elementary and high school age students may participate in overnight trips, such as retreats or field trips to places of historical significance such as Washington, D.C. The standard permission form should be used. Chaperones should have notarized medical releases for the young persons, which allow the procurement of medical attention for injured or ill participants. In light of increasing concern for liability, it is not unusual for hospital personnel to decline to do anything beyond immediate measures until a parent or guardian can arrive.

The permission form should clearly state the penalties to be imposed if rules are broken. For example, violations of civil law and use of alcohol or drugs probably should result in a participant's being sent home. The permission form might include a statement such as, "We/I agree to arrange transportation home for (name of child) in the event of serious infractions of a rule or rules."

At the high school level, trips to foreign countries are also a concern. Campus or youth ministers may take young people to World Youth Day or have a third-world experience. Only reputable companies who can provide proof of insurance should be allowed to administer such trips. A religious educator or minister must understand that if the parish or school advertises the trip and supplies the adult supervisors who chaperone the trip, the parish or school cannot evade its responsibility for the trip; in effect, the trip is a parish- or school-sponsored trip.

Religious educators and ministers frequently ask about the possibility of parents being entirely responsible for trips with the parish or school having no responsibility for what happens on those trips. If the adult leaders allow fundraising in the parish program or school, dissemination of materials about the trip, etc., a court could well find that the trip is school- or parish-sponsored.

Finally, the decision to take an off-campus trip is one that should not be made lightly. The wise decision-maker weighs the risks and benefits posed by the trip before making a final determination.

Confidentiality

One of the more perplexing situations facing ministers and educators today is that presented by young people's sharing of confidential information. Although people of any age can share confidences, it seems that today's young people may well face more pressures and problems than young people of any other decade. Pastors and other administrators may have heard stories about teachers who failed to report student threats and the student subsequently acted on the threat. The responsibility for receiving the confidences of young people and advising students in both day-to-day situations and crises can be overwhelming. Busy catechists and parish staff members may well ask, "What am I supposed to do? I know I'm not a professional counselor, a psychiatrist, or a social worker, but I'm the one the individual trusts, the one that was consulted. Are there certain legal issues involved in the receiving of confidences? Is there matter that must be made known to others, even when the person has asked for and received a promise of confidentiality from me?"

These are good questions to ask. Staff members cannot afford to think that they can help all persons all the time, for such is not possible. If, for example, a student were to come to a teacher or catechist and say that he or she is experiencing shortness of breath and chest pain, the adult would quickly summon both the student's parents and medical assistance. Yet, psychological problems are no less serious than physical ones, and the layperson who attempts to deal with such problems unaided may well be courting tragedy for both self and the one confiding.

Confidentiality is generally held to mean that one individual or several individuals will keep private information that has been given to them, and will not reveal it. For example, the person who receives the sacrament of reconciliation rightfully expects that the subject matter of confession will be held sacred by the confessor and will not be revealed to anyone. Indeed, there are accounts of priests who died rather than break the seal of confession.

Friends share confidences with each other. One individual may say to another, "This is confidential; you cannot repeat it." The person speaking in confidence has a right to expect that the confidant to whom the information has been given will keep the matter secret. But there are recognized limits to what friends will keep private. If one's friend confides that she has been stockpiling sleeping medication and plans to take all of it that evening so as to commit suicide, it is not hard to see that morality demands that the confidant communicate that knowledge to a spouse or other family member of the confiding individual, or take some other action that would intervene in the attempted suicide.

It is not unheard of for an adult who would not hesitate to get help for a friend to believe that a young person who is talking about suicide is not serious, or can be talked out of the planned action, or is not capable of carrying out a threatened suicide. As child and adolescent psychologists report, young people often do not think through the long-term ramifications of suicide attempts. There is also, among some young people, a fascination with death, as can be seen by the idolization of famous people who have died young or committed suicide.

If a student tells a teacher, catechist or youth minister that he or she is going to harm self or others, the adult must reveal that information, even if a promise of confidentiality has been given. In a number of lawsuits brought against teachers and school districts, parents sought damages from teachers who were told by students in confidence that they planned to harm themselves or others; the teachers did not contact parents or other authorities. In some cases, the educators were brought to trial on a claim of negligence by failure to warn.

School shootings and related violence have resulted in a flurry of litigation. Parents of victims have brought suit against the school district, the schools, administrators and teachers; some suits allege that the journals and writings of the perpetrators contained warning signals that staff members disregarded. The litigation may continue for years; regardless of which side "wins," the case fallout will be enormous in terms of student and community trust. Such cases should also cause DREs, catechists, campus and youth ministers and pastors to question the wisdom of journal-writing and, indeed, any writing that may involve personal thoughts and feelings.

Counselor Immunity

It is a widely held myth that counselors, physicians, psychologists, and social workers have legal immunity from responsibility for any injuries that may arise from failing to act on confidential information presented to them. Most states have abolished counselor immunity, and the few who still "have it on the books" have imposed several limitations on the concept. A counselor who hears from a person that the individual plans to kill his or her parents and does nothing about it will not be legally able to decline to answer questions under oath, nor will the counselor be held harmless for any resulting injuries if he or she decides not to reveal the threats. Counselors, catechists and other ministers must make it very clear to a confiding individual that they will keep confidences unless the individual's health, life or safety or those of another person are threatened. Administrators should seriously consider the development of a policy that directs adult staff members to tell individuals at the outset, "I will keep your confidences so long as no one's life, health, or safety is involved. Once life, health, or safety is involved, I cannot promise confidentiality." The only two privileges from disclosure of confidential information, which seem to remain in state law, are that of priest/penitent and attorney/client. Even the husband/wife privilege that allowed a spouse to refuse to testify against a spouse has been largely abandoned.

In light of the above, catechists and ministers must presume that no legal protection exists for those who receive confidences. What can be expected of a catechist or minister who wants to be a role model for young persons, who wants to be approachable and helpful? The answer is simple: Lay down the ground rules for confidentiality before receiving any confidences. If an anyone asks to talk to a catechist or minister in confidence, that adult should reiterate the ground rules before the sharing begins.

Journal Writing

In religion, language arts, English and other subjects, teachers have long recognized the value of student journal writing. Today, many ministries utilize a journal approach. This practice does, however, carry a real risk of disclosure of information that the minister is compelled to reveal. All must set the same rules for confidentiality discussed above.

Today adults must understand that they *are* expected to read what students write. If an adult is doing the writing and shares it with a minister, the minister is bound to report any behaviors that could result in injury. If a person cannot read the assignment, then the assignment should not be given. In particular, staff members should avoid such techniques as telling students to clip together pages they do not wish the adult to read or to write at the top of such pages, "Please do not read." Journal writing has a place in today's communities, but the supervising adults must be sure that all participants understand the parameters of the assignment and of the responsibilities for reporting threats and danger. Parish leaders, catechists, and ministers should discuss the concept of journaling and develop policies and procedures to ensure that journals are used appropriately.

It is not uncommon for campus and youth ministry programs, as well as religious education programs, to ask students to keep prayer journals. The general rule of thumb is the adult should read what the student or participant has written. If the journal is to be only between the writer and God, the supervisor should communicate in writing to the parents the nature of the assignment and the fact that he/she will not be reading entries.

Retreats

The retreat experience is extremely important for persons of all ages. However, young people in particular are often at their most vulnerable in such situations. They may share stories of child abuse, sexual harassment, family dysfunction, and even possible criminal activity. While encouraging sharing, the group leader must once again set the ground rules before the sharing begins. The use of peer leaders does not lessen the responsibility of the supervising adults. Student leaders must be told of the ground rules and of the necessity to communicate them to group members as well as procedures to be followed in notifying adults if matter is revealed that must be reported.

The standard of care for supervising adults is obviously less than it is for supervising children and adolescents. Nonetheless, failure to share information about potential harm can result in legal liability for the non-reporting minister.

Case Law

In the case, *Brooks v. Logan and Joint District No. 2*, (1995), parents of a student who committed suicide filed an action for wrongful death and a claim for negligent infliction of emotional distress against a teacher who had assigned the keeping of journals to her class. Jeff Brooks was a student at Meridian High School and was assigned to Ms. Logan's English class. Students were asked to make entries into a daily journal as part of their English composition work. For a period of four months prior to his death, Jeff wrote in his journal.

After his death, Ms. Logan read through the entries and gave the journal to a school counselor, who delivered it to Jeff's parents. Jeff had made journal entries that indicated that he was depressed and that he was contemplating suicide. One entry read as follows:

> Well, Edgar Allen Poe [sic], I can live with studying about that stuff he wrote especially the one short story about the evil eye.... I used to write poems until I pronounced myself dead in one of them and how could I write poems or stories if I was dead....
>
> Recently ... see I went into a medium depression and wrote poems to two special people.... I told them it was too bad that I had to say goodby this way (like that) but it would be the only way and I felt better.... (p. 81)

Ms. Logan maintained that Jeff had requested that she not read his entries, so that he would feel free to express himself. The journal contained a note in which Ms. Logan stated that she would not read the journal for content, but would only check for dates and length. The parents maintained that, in a conversation with Ms. Logan after their receipt of the journal, she stated that she had "reread the entries." Ms. Logan denied that she made that statement, and contends that she did not read the entries in question until after Jeff's death.

The lower court granted summary judgment in favor of the teacher and the school district. However, the appellate court reversed the finding, and held that there were issues of fact in existence, which could only be determined at trial. Thus, a trial court was directed to determine whether Ms. Logan's actions or inactions constituted negligence contributing to Jeff's death. The court was directed to make a determination as to whether Jeff's suicide was foreseeable: would a reasonable person in Ms. Logan's place have recognized the possibility of suicide and notified someone? The appellate court refers to similar case law in which jailers have been held liable for the suicide of prisoners when the prisoners had exhibited warning signs.

This case and the discussion indicate the vulnerability of teachers and any adult who receive student confidences. DRE's and parish ministers should discuss the topic of confidentiality with their staffs and adopt policies that will support a legally sound approach to confidentiality. The wise minister will establish and enforce ground rules for dealing with student confidences, and will seek help from others when appropriate.

Adult/Young Person Relationships

Ministers, DREs, catechists and other staff members care about young people, and that concern can extend to many areas of life. Adults often find themselves counseling students in personal matters; it is not unusual for a teacher, catechist, campus or youth minister to find himself or herself in the position of "surrogate parent." Young people often entrust adults with confidential information. Paid and volunteer staff members, many with little training in professional counseling, often question what is appropriate in interacting with students/participants outside the classroom or ministerial setting.

Few guidelines are available. Teachers and other personnel often deal with situations that pose personal and legal risks for the adults as well as for the students. In some situations, parents have threatened and/or pursued legal action against a teacher whose actions they viewed as unwise, inappropriate, sexually motivated or interfering with the parent/child relationship. All adults working in the educational ministry of the Church should be aware of the legal ramifications involved in adult/young person relationships, and be careful to avoid the perception as well as the reality of inappropriateness.

Sexual Misconduct

One end of the student/staff relationship spectrum is represented by sexual misconduct. Sexual misconduct *can* be alleged in apparently innocent situations. Students *can* misinterpret touching, and an educator could find himself or herself facing child abuse charges. Extreme caution is in order whenever an adult touches a student.

Another kind of problem is posed by a young person who believes that a supervising adult has not responded to efforts to achieve a closer relationship and thus may accuse an educator or minister of inappropriate conduct as a retaliatory measure. Serious consequences can result from an allegation of child abuse, even if that allegation is eventually proved false. At the very least, such a false allegation is extremely embarrassing for the adult. If a child abuse report is made, authorities will question the adult and the alleged victim. Thus, it is imperative that adults protect themselves and the students they teach by practicing appropriate behavior with students.

Fear of teachers' facing child abuse allegations has caused some public school districts in this country to adopt rules that prohibit any faculty touching of students. Such rules preclude putting one's arm around students, patting a student on the back, and giving a student a hug. No educator would want to adopt such a position, but common sense precautions must be taken for the protection of all.

Avoiding the Appearance of Impropriety: Recommendations for Keeping Boundaries

Today everyone seems to be talking about boundaries and the avoidance of litigation prompted by the appearance of impropriety. In response to many requests, here is a "don'ts" list for religious educators and ministers.

1. *Do not stay alone in a room with a student unless there is a window permitting others to view the room or the door is open.*

    Think before you act. Ask yourself how someone else might perceive what you are doing. If a student were to leave your classroom or other area and claim abuse, a closed area with no visual access would leave little room for a defense.

2. *Do not allow students to become overly friendly or familiar with you. Students should not call religious educators or ministers by their first names or nick names.*

   There is a difference between being "friendly" and being "friends" with students. Boundaries between adults and young persons must be enforced. Insisting on proper titles is one way to keep boundaries.

3. *Do not engage in private correspondence with students. If you receive personal communication from a student and the communication is not appropriate, keep a copy of the communication and do not respond unless you have received permission from a supervisor.*

   It is not uncommon for students to develop "crushes" on religious educators and ministers, to fantasize about them, and/or to try to communicate on a peer level. If one receives student letters, etc. that are romantic, sexual, or otherwise inappropriate, it is best not to respond and to report the occurrence to one's supervisor for everyone's protection.

4. *Do not visit students in their homes unless their parents are present.*

   Being alone with young persons can give an appearance of impropriety. Many instances of sexual abuse are alleged to have occurred when adults were present in a student's home when the parents were absent. In particular, if there is no one home but the student, the situation can quickly become one of your word against the student's.

5. *Do not invite students to your home.*

   The comments in number four also apply here.

6. *Do not transport students in your vehicle.*

   Obviously, there exists the same problematic situation of an adult being alone with a student or students. Additionally, the adult may assume personal liability for any accident or injury. It can be very tempting to respond to a student's request for a ride home, but a better approach would be to wait in an open area with the student until transportation arrives or to direct the student to a parish leader.

7. *Do not take the role of surrogate parent with a student.*

   Religious educators and ministers are not parents and do not have the responsibilities or privileges of parents. While being supportive and helpful, Church leaders must respect the rights of parents. Some parents, feeling they have been displaced in their children's affections by teachers, are seeking restraining orders against the educators.

8. *Do not criticize a student's parents to the student.*

    No matter how poorly parents act, they are most likely the only parents their children will have. If you believe a child is abused or neglected, contact the appropriate authorities.

9. *Do not give students your home phone number without the permission and knowledge of your supervisor.*

    Communicating with students via telephone on a regular basis and/or encouraging students to call you at home can give an appearance, even if not the reality, of impropriety. It is best to call students from the school or parish phones if possible.

10. *Do not communicate with students from your home e-mail address.*

    E-mail was the topic of a November, 2003 *NCEA News Notes* article and readers may want to refer to it. In brief, communicating with students from home e-mail addresses can give an appearance of secrecy. Religious educators and ministers should always use their parish e-mail accounts.

11. *Do not hire students to work in your home without the express knowledge and consent of your supervisor.*

    Mixing roles is generally not a good idea. Acting as a young person's employer while serving as a catechist or campus/youth minister can "muddy" the waters where boundaries are concerned. For example, a male teacher taking a babysitter home at midnight is placing himself in a particularly vulnerable position should the student make a claim of inappropriate conduct. Additionally, adults can incur liability for injuries students sustain while in their employ.

Ask yourself: How would I feel if what I am doing were to appear on the front page of the paper tomorrow?

Many problems could be avoided if adults would ask themselves this question before certain interactions with young people. An even better question might be, "Would Jesus do this?" Fidelity to prayer and the exercise of common sense can help educators avoid boundary "pitfalls" and can protect everyone.

Boundaries

The events of the past two years concerning sexual abuse in the Catholic Church have taken a heavy toll on all who minister in Catholic education. People are afraid, and there is reason for fear. Fear can be a healthy thing, if it helps people recognize danger and act appropriately. Fire is a good thing, but children learn early in life that if you get too close to a fire, you can get burned. Relationships between adults and students are good, but like fire, they must be kept within certain boundaries; if they are not, the damage that can result may be catastrophic. Catechists and ministers should not be paralyzed because of the allegations of sexual abuse and the upheaval they have brought. Rather, they should view the situation as a "wake up call" to re-examine how they deal with the children and young people entrusted to their care. This section will discuss the parameters that should encompass adult/young person relationships and will include an excellent set of "Guidelines for Ministry" that are in place at Providence High School in Burbank, California. These guidelines may be helpful in promoting discussion of the sensitive topics of relationships and boundaries.

Religious educators and youth/campus ministers care about students. That care extends to all areas of a student's life. Religious educators may find themselves counseling students in personal matters; it is not unusual to find yourself in the position of surrogate parent or counselor, a position that is fraught with possibilities for misunderstanding and misperception. Students often entrust catechists and ministers with confidential information. Catechists may, with little training in professional counseling, often question what is appropriate in interacting with students both inside and outside the classroom setting.

Few definitive guidelines have been available. Catechists and other personnel may deal with situations that pose personal and legal risks for the adults as well as the students. One boundary problem results when a parent believes that an adult has so insinuated him or herself into the child's life that there is no room left for the parent. Parents may object to what they view as a "too close" relationship between their child and a Church worker; even the parent who rarely, if ever, makes an appearance at Church events may object if he or she feels that the catechist or campus/youth minister has taken on the role of the parent. It is important for all adults to understand that they are not the students' parents, however much a particular young person might wish otherwise. There are more than a few situations in which parents have threatened and/or pursued legal action against a teacher whose actions they have viewed as unwise, inappropriate, sexually motivated, or just intrusive.

All who minister in the Catholic Church must avoid even the appearance of impropriety. Perception far too easily is viewed as reality. A reputation is almost impossible to rebuild as people often remember the accusation, but not the exoneration. It is far better to avoid being accused in the first place than to successfully defend one's self against an accusation of impropriety. Many people still believe in the old adage, "Where there is smoke, there is fire," and many exonerated persons find they simply cannot be effective in ministry after an accusation.

The topic of boundaries gets much attention today. Catechists and ministers want to be interested in the lives of their students and they often establish close relationships with them. Yet, even the closest of relationships must have boundaries. Sometimes, well-meaning persons get "too close" to others. People may share personal information and answer any questions put to them. Far from being open, they are destroying the boundaries that the young person needs. A teacher does not need to answer every question put to him or her by a young person. For example, one should decline to answer questions such as, "Did you sleep with your husband/wife before you were married?" "Did you ever smoke dope?" "Are you gay?" Boundaries are healthy and personal boundaries help keep us within appropriate legal and professional boundaries.

Parish leaders must understand that they are professionals rendering a service. Just as a counselor or psychiatrist is professionally bound to avoid emotional involvement with a client, we should strive to avoid becoming so emotionally involved with a student that objectivity and fairness are compromised. Catechists and ministers must remember that they have many students who need them and their attention. If a relationship with a student keeps the parish staff person from responding to other needs on a regular basis, then one should seriously examine the appropriateness of the relationship. Those who work with another adult who is exhibiting questionable judgment in relationships with students have clear legal and moral responsibilities to challenge the individual to examine his or her behavior and its potential effects. In seeking to assess the appropriateness of an adult/ student relationship, some mental health professionals recommend asking one's self such questions as: Whose needs are being met? Is there a boundary? Where is it?

In the wake of the stunning number of allegations of sexual abuse against priests and other ministers, it is important for DREs, campus and youth ministers to carefully monitor the ministerial setting. If the supervisor is disturbed by someone's words or actions, he or she should immediately discuss the situation with the parties involved. If one has a "funny feeling," one should not ignore it, but should ask questions. If something does not feel right or causes discomfort, there is probably cause for concern. It is too easy for anyone, with the best intentions in the world, to become emotionally involved with students.

One reason situations can escalate into serious, even tragic, outcomes is because people hesitate to say anything without proof. As in most other situations, approach is everything. One does not have to make allegations; the supervisor can state that he or she has become aware of a situation that could eventually cause problems for the individual and can involve the person in a discussion of the situation and possible courses of action. Everyone involved should be grateful that the supervisor cares enough to monitor what takes place and to protect the legal rights and good name of all. Catechists and ministers concerned about the behavior of another adult should express that concern to the individual. If the concerns are not addressed, they must be shared with an supervisor.

Additional Guidelines

Occasionally, a policy or handbook is so good that it is appropriate for a wider audience. The following "Guidelines for Ministry to Minors" is one such case. Ministers and catechists may find these particularly helpful and they are presented from Burbank, California's *Providence High School Faculty Handbook*. While these guidelines are written for high school teachers, the content is appropriate for all involved in ministry to young people.

Guidelines for Ministry to Minors

1. Minors should always be viewed, whether in a social or ministerial situation, as the "restricted individuals" they are, that is, they are not independent. Wherever they go and whatever they do should be with the explicit knowledge of the parents or guardian. Also, they are subject to specific civil laws, which may prohibit certain activities. They are not adults and are not permitted unfettered decisions. Any and all involvement should be approached from this premise.

2. Caution and professional attitudes are to be observed in all interactions with minors.

3. Another person should be present in situations involving a minor *whenever possible*.

4. Games or sport activities should be engaged in only with the presence of other persons or in a place openly accessible and visible to others.

5. Faculty and staff should avoid being present as the only other person in a locker room or other dressing area when a minor is using the facilities.

6. Student trips should have a sufficient number of adult chaperones to preclude the appearance of inappropriate personal involvement with students.

7. While on trips, adults should maintain a professional demeanor and socialize with the utmost discretion and the highest professional standards and in the presence of other reputable adult chaperones.

8. There should never be any trip with a minor alone, most especially any overnight trip.

9. Staff members and chaperones should never stay overnight in the same room with a minor, even if there are two beds. Exception: a parent and his/her child could share the same room.

10. Attraction to or from minors should be recognized and care taken in all interactions. A supervisor should be notified of any such attraction immediately.

11. It is absolutely forbidden for any member of the staff to date a student or participant.

12. Adults should always be aware of the "power" of their role and position, which can be a very seductive force.

13. Discussions of a sexual nature are to take place only in an educational context as part of a specific curriculum or in an official counseling context. Sexual terms and innuendo must be avoided when interacting with young people.

14. Topics or vocabulary, which could not comfortably be used in the presence of parents or administrators, should not be employed with students.

15. Adults may never supply or serve alcohol or any controlled substance to minors.

16. Alcohol should never be consumed in the presence of minors nor should it be used if activities with minors are scheduled.

17. Finally, all adults should regard themselves as representatives of Christ when dealing with the students who are part of their charge and should treat each student with respect and care.

Jesus' Gospel statement that it is better for you to have a millstone wrapped around your neck and be buried in the bottom of the sea than to lead one of these little ones astray should be a sobering reminder to all adults who minister to youth. There can be no more sacred trust than being charged with the care of the souls of the young.

E-Mail

E-mail and instant messaging are examples of the blessing and the curse that technology brings to parishes and schools. Everyone must understand that there is no privacy on the Internet. The same boundary issues that must be respected in oral communications must be respected in written ones, particularly when e-mail is involved. Many people may view what is written, so the test of publicity must always be kept in mind: how would I feel if this correspondence suddenly ended up on the front page of the newspaper or on the evening news? The following ten guidelines can guide administrators and staff in the appropriate use of e-mail.

1. Use your school or parish e-mail account. Never use your home or personal e-mail account. Using a personal account can give an appearance of secrecy. If you do not have access to a school or parish account, set up a separate account on your home computer and use it only for matters related to your ministry.

2. Always remember you are a professional or adult volunteer rendering a service. You are not the young person's friend or buddy.

3. Communicate only about matters that are appropriate to be discussed in the parish or school. Most especially avoid any communication that might be construed as having sexual overtones. Do not reply to any such e-mail you receive; make and keep a copy of any such inappropriate communication and notify your supervisor.

4. Write as though you are certain that others will read what you write. Remember that a young person can share your message with others by a simple push of a button.

5. Remember there is no such thing as a private e-mail.

6. Do not use instant messaging. While it may have become customary for those who work in youth ministry to use instant messaging to communicate details regarding a program or gathering due to the fast pace, high mobility and independence of young people, ministers would be advised to proceed with caution. If used in the course of ministry, instant messages should originate from a parish account, not the minister's home account. It would be better not to put young people to whom you minister on your "buddy list." If you find that someone has added you to

his or her list, ask that your name be removed and keep a written record of your request. Remember—people can make copies of instant messages and they can come back to haunt you.

7. Ask yourself, if anyone asked to see this communication, would I be embarrassed by what I have written? If the answer is "yes," don't send the e-mail.

8. Remember—the young person you are e-mailing is someone's child. How would you feel if your son or daughter received the e-mail you are about to send? If you think your e-mail might somehow be misunderstood, don't send it.

9. Remember—boundaries must be respected in written correspondence as well as in oral communication. Don't push the boundaries of ministerial relationships.

10. Finally, e-mail can be misinterpreted. Before sending an e-mail, ask yourself if someone reading it might "read something into it" that you didn't intend or if your message might be misinterpreted. Communicate in person whenever possible.

Negligence: What Is It? How Can We Avoid It?

The reality of sexual abuse cases in the Catholic Church raises the fear level of most persons who work in Catholic schools and other ministries. Catechists and ministers rightfully fear both the inconvenience and the expense of litigation. If a DRE, campus/youth minister is sued, there is a high degree of probability that the suit will allege negligence. Negligence is often the most difficult type of case about which to predict an accurate judicial outcome. What may be considered negligence in one court may not be so considered in another. It is much better, obviously, to avoid being accused of negligence in the first place than to take one's chances on the outcome of a lawsuit.

Those who work in ministries with young people are often misinformed about some of the greatest problem areas. While sexual abuse cases claim the headlines, the vast majority of cases involving Catholic parishes and schools are not ones alleging sexual abuse; rather, the most often-litigated cases are ones alleging negligence. *Black's Law Dictionary* defines negligence as, "the failure to use such care as a reasonably prudent and careful person would use under similar circumstances; it is the doing of some act which a person of ordinary prudence would not have done under similar circumstances or failure to do what a person of ordinary prudence would have done under similar circumstances." Thus, there are two types of negligence: *omission*, the failure to do what should have been done, and *commission*, the doing of something that led to an injury. This section will discuss the legal concept of negligence and some case law concerning negligence. The cases are ones that arose in schools; however, it is easy to apply the principles of each case to other areas of ministry such as religious education and youth ministry. While non-school cases in the Catholic Church used to be almost non-existent, they are on the rise. Everyone who works with young persons needs to learn the lessons of negligence law.

Catechists, for example, rather than DREs, are more likely to be present when something goes wrong or someone is injured, and a lawsuit is filed. Pastors and administrators can find themselves named in lawsuits as well, under the doctrine of *respondeat superior*, let the superior answer. This doctrine allows courts to hold the superiors of negligent persons liable for the employee or volunteer's negligence. Courts expect that all supervisors will have instructed their employees and volunteers, who are their agents, in appropriate behavior. Employees and volunteers have a right to expect that they will be given the information they need to avoid negligence. Adults have a responsibility as well to use common sense and to act the way one would expect a reasonable, mature adult charged with the supervision of young people to act. Courts also expect that policies and procedures will be in place, and that staff will be familiar with those policies and procedures and will follow them.

All religious educators and ministers should be familiar with the elements of negligence. Four elements must be present before a finding of legal negligence can be made: duty, violation of duty, proximate cause and injury. If one of these elements is missing, legal negligence cannot be found. Since negligence is an unintentional act which results in an injury, a person charged with negligence is generally not going to face criminal charges or spend time in prison. An examination of each of the four elements necessary to constitute a finding of negligence should be helpful.

Duty

The first element is duty. Young people have a right to safety, and adult catechists and ministers have a responsibility to protect the safety of all entrusted to their care. Adults are expected to provide reasonable supervision of young people. Parish leaders should develop rules and regulations, which guide employees and volunteers in providing for safe environments.

Staff members will generally not be held responsible for injuries occurring at a place where, or at a time when, they had no responsibility. If a youth minister is walking through a mall on Sunday afternoon and sees two students fighting, he has no duty to intervene since he is not part of the mall security force. However, concern for his students, or for the reputation of the parish may prompt him to intervene in an attempt to stop the fight. He may feel he has a moral or legal obligation to intervene. Once he takes action, he has assumed a duty he was not leally required to assume.

When considering the concept of duty, it is important to keep in mind that the court will look at the reasonableness of the adult's behavior. A commonly asked question is, Did the person do what a reasonable person in the same situation would be expected to do?

Violation of Duty

The second element is violation of duty. Negligence cannot exist if the supervising educator has not violated a duty. Courts expect that accidents and spontaneous actions can occur. For example, if a teacher is properly supervising a playground at recess, and one child throws a rock at another child and causes an injury, the teacher cannot be held liable if she had no reason to know or suspect that the child was likely to throw a rock. However, if a teacher who is responsible for the supervision of the playground were to allow rock throwing to continue without attempting to stop it and a student were injured, the teacher would probably be held liable. Similarly, a teacher who leaves a classroom unattended in order to take a coffee break will generally be held to have violated a duty. But if it can be demonstrated that teachers have, as a general practice, taken coffee breaks and left classes unattended, and, because of the inattention or inaction of the principal, nothing was done about the situation, the principal may be held equally, if not more, liable than the teacher.

If a catechist takes a group of six-year-olds to a lake and leaves them unsupervised for an hour, her action would be viewed as professional negligence. Nonetheless, if no injury results from the person's action, as will be discussed later, there can be no finding of legal negligence. Thus, legal negligence must be distinguished from professional negligence, which is definitely demonstrated by leaving children unattended. Courts expect that persons will take reasonable precautions to ensure that accidents will not happen. Courts have consistently said that there is no requirement that the specific type of accident be foreseen, but merely that the possibility of some danger should have been foreseen. However, violation of duty in one instance may not result in a finding of legal negligence if a causal connection, or proximate cause, between the violation and the injury cannot be shown or if no injury was incurred.

Proximate Cause

The third element of negligence is proximate cause. Proximate cause is a contributing factor that "makes or breaks" a negligence claim. If the supervisor had done what should have been done, there would have been no injury, or if the supervisor had not done the thing that was done, there would have been no injury. The "old" but still very relevant case of *Levandoski v. Jackson City School District* 328 So.2d 339 (Minn. 1976) illustrates. A teacher failed to report a student as missing from her class. The student was later found murdered some distance from the school. She had also been sexually assaulted. The child's mother alleged that if the absence had been properly and promptly reported the murder could have been prevented. Clearly, the teacher had a duty to know who was present and to report those who should have been present and were not. She violated that duty. The court ruled, nonetheless, that the mother had failed to prove that had the absence been reported, the assault and murder could have been prevented. Thus, the claim failed for a lack of proximate cause. One should not conclude that carelessness in reporting absences is not a serious matter. If the facts were changed to a situation in which the student was found murdered on the school grounds or in the school building, a different judgment might have been given since it would be much more likely that the report might have prevented the injuries.

One of the most well-known Catholic school negligence cases is *Smith v. the Archbishop of St. Louis*, 632 S.W.2d 516 (Mo. Ct. App. 1982). A second grade teacher kept a lighted candle to honor the Blessed Mother on her desk during the month of May. She admitted under oath that she gave the children no special instructions regarding candles and/or fires. On a day during which a play was to be presented, the Smith child, wearing a crepe paper costume, walked too close to the flame. Her costume caught on fire, and she was severely injured, particularly in the facial area. Her scars and disfigurement are permanent. The child sustained psychological damage and experts testified that she would likely experience a lifetime of psychological problems. The teacher sustained serious burns to her hands when she attempted to extinguish the flames. The court awarded the student damages to compensate both medical costs and pain and suffering. Maintaining that the injuries were an accident, the archdiocese's insurer argued against damages beyond the medical costs. The court disagreed, and let stand a jury verdict against the diocese. The teacher was dismissed as a defendant early in the proceedings, but the archdiocese remained a defendant, primarily because it had the resources to pay a judgment.

Clearly, the teacher's violation of duty in placing a lighted candle within reach of seven-year-olds was a contributing factor and constituted proximate cause. Although this case happened in a Catholic school, a person can easily see how such a situation could occur in religious education, youth ministry, retreat and other settings.

The *Smith* case illustrates the concept of **foreseeability**. The plaintiff did not have to prove that the defendant could foresee that a *particular* injury (plaintiff's costume catching fire) had to occur; the plaintiff had to establish that a reasonable person would have foreseen that injuries *could* result from having a lighted candle in a second grade classroom, particularly when no safety instructions had been given to the students. In determining whether a teacher's behavior was reasonable, a court might ask the following questions: 1. Had the teacher given the students clear instructions as to how to behave in his or her absence? 2. Is the teacher absent a reasonable length of time? Five minutes seem reasonable; a thirty-minute absence during which a teacher took a coffee break, made a phone call, or copied papers would probably not be considered reasonable.

In determining whether a supervisor might be liable for accidents occurring during a staff member's absence, a court might pose these questions: (1) Has the supervisor developed a clear policy for those who need to leave classrooms or other areas? (2) Has he or she implemented the policy? (3) Has he or she supervised persons to make sure that they are following policy? From the above discussion, it should be apparent that negligence is a complex concept. It is often difficult to predict what a court will consider proximate cause in any particular allegation of negligence.

Injury

The fourth element of negligence is injury. No matter how irresponsible the behavior, if there is no injury, there can be no legal negligence. This reality is surprising to some people. The purpose of litigation is to be made whole, restored to as similar a condition existing prior to the injury as possible. Injuries do not have to be physical; they can be psychological, mental, academic, etc. as well. Many cases do not allege physical injury, but seek damages for emotional distress, particularly when that distress can be demonstrated. There are two causes of action alleging emotional distress. One is negligent infliction of emotional distress which generally requires that there be physical symptoms of emotional distress. Intentional infliction of emotional distress, while harder to prove, of course, does not require physical manifestations of the distress.

If a teacher or other adult does something that fits all four requirements of legal negligence, and the action (or inaction) "shocks the conscience of the court," a finding of gross negligence can be made. Such a finding generally results in punitive or exemplary damages which are intended to punish the institution and hold it up as an example to others of what not to do.

The younger the child, the greater is the responsibility. It might be acceptable to leave a group of high school seniors alone for a good reason when it would not be acceptable to leave a group of first graders alone. It is reasonable to expect that fifteen-year-olds of average intelligence could observe traffic signals when crossing a street. It would not be reasonable to expect kindergarten children to do so.

Thus, the concept of negligence is both simple and complex. Common sense is often the best guide for behavior. While the outcomes of negligence cases can be hard to predict, the person who can demonstrate foresight and vigilance with regard to student safety will have a sound defense if competence and care are ever questioned.

Being Proactive: Preventing Injuries

The beginning of the academic year and regular intervals throughout the year are good times to review potential hazards and dangerous practices in the areas under one's supervision. Staff members can contribute to the overall safety of the school or parish by giving thought to the following questions and discussing their responses and findings with the appropriate persons.

(1) Are there any hazardous conditions in my classroom or other area(s)? If yes, can I eliminate them on my own? If I cannot, do I know whom to contact and how to record the conditions and actions taken?

(2) Have I noticed any hazardous conditions in the building or on the school or parish grounds? Whom should I inform? If the condition is not corrected, then I need to document that fact and notify my superior.

(3) Have I noticed any patterns of dangerous behavior among the young people I supervise? What steps can I take to lessen, if not completely eliminate, these behaviors? Are my rules clear and

consistently enforced? Do I understand it is more important for students to be safe than to have their own way? If I do, do I make decisions based on student safety first?

(4) Have I ever observed suspicious persons in or around the building? Have I reported these observations to my supervisor? Are signs directing visitors to the office clearly in evidence? Do people obey the signs?

(5) Is there any situation that makes me uncomfortable? If yes, why am I uncomfortable? Should I discuss this with the pastor, principal, DRE, youth or campus minister? When in doubt, it is always better to err on the side of caution.

Chapter Four

Bishops, Pastors, Councils and Boards: Rights and Responsibilities

A s stated earlier in this text, two systems of law govern Catholic parishes, programs and schools: civil law of the country, state, city, etc. and Canon Law, the law of the Catholic Church. Civil courts, respecting the First Amendment's guarantee of the free exercise of religion, will generally not interfere in the internal affairs of religious institutions. Civil law recognizes the right of religious organizations to govern themselves. This right, however, is not absolute. Civil courts will not allow religious institutions to evade legal responsibilities by "hiding behind" Church law. Within the wide parameter imposed by civil law, though, churches have significant autonomy.

Canon Law governs both the existence and continuance of Catholic institutions. An institution, such as a Catholic high school or parish can call itself Catholic only with the approval of the bishop. The bishop has the duty to inspect schools and parishes as well as the right to appoint and remove teachers of religion. Traditionally, it has been said that all Catholic schools are subject to their bishops in matters of faith and morals and in all other matters prescribed by the Church's *Code of Canon Law.*

The bishop has final responsibility for all Church laws in his diocese. He may, and generally does, delegate much of his power to other persons in the diocese, such as directors, superintendents, the vicar, diocesan boards and similar bodies. Although he may delegate power, he can never delegate responsibility. Mirroring the civil law theory of *respondeat superior*, the bishop can be required to answer in Canon Law for the actions of his designates.

The Canon Law equivalent of a civil corporation is the "juridic person," an individual legal entity recognized by the Church. Schools may be either separate juridic persons or part of the juridic person of another entity such as a parish or religious congregation. Although a thorough consideration of Canon Law is beyond the scope of this text, it may be helpful to examine briefly the four most common types of Catholic schools operating in the country today since religious educators and campus/youth ministers may operate within schools or in cooperation with them.

The first type is the parish elementary or high school that operates as part of a parish governed by a pastor who is the ultimate authority in the parish, subject only to the bishop. It is important for everyone associated with a Catholic school to understand that its governance is not a democracy. As the bishop has the final responsibility for the diocese, so the pastor has the final responsibility for the parish, limited only by the bishop's right to review. The pastor probably shares his decision-making with many persons and entities in the parish. One would hope that he operates in a collegial spirit. However, he stands alone in a very real sense under Canon Law in his ultimate responsibility for the decisions that guide the life of his parish, programs and the school.

More recently, changing demographics and declining enrollments in some dioceses, as well as strategic planning efforts, have resulted in the development of the regional school, often a consolidation of two or more schools. Governance structures may take different forms in these schools. In some, one pastor or an individual designated by the bishop as the parochial vicar may have the final responsibility; in others, there may be a shared decision-making structure among the pastors of the parishes supporting the school.

A third type of school, the diocesan school, has long been associated with secondary education. In more recent times, some dioceses have begun to sponsor diocesan regional elementary and middle schools. These schools are not necessarily affiliated with parishes. Different governance models, including governance by a board directly under the jurisdiction of the bishop, may be employed. The question of the regional school as a juridic person or part of a juridic person must be resolved under the direction of the bishop. Today, it is not uncommon to find multi-parish regional religious education and/or youth ministry programs following much the same model as the regional school.

A fourth type of school is one operated by a religious congregation or other independent body, such as a board of trustees. Religious congregations and trustees are not generally as directly related to dioceses, as are the members of governing structures of other schools. The independent school may be a juridic person in its own right or it may be part of the juridic person represented by a religious congregation in the diocese.

The independent school owned by a Board of Trustees is much more common today than it was in 1995 when the first edition of this text appeared. In one scenario, a religious congregation owned the school and decided, usually in the face of limited finances and dwindling vocations, to withdraw overall financial support from the school. Congregations may have sold the school to a board of trustees with the provision that the property would revert to the religious congregation if the school closed. Like the other types of schools discussed above, these schools are subject to the bishop's authority in matters of faith and morals. Independent Catholic schools and their board members must understand and accept the bishop's authority in these matters; to attempt to act in a manner contrary to the wishes and directives of the bishop could place a school or a parish's programs at risk.

There are also some independent schools that have dropped the word "Catholic" from their official titles. Literature may identify such a school as, for example, "Sts. Augustine and Monica School, an independent school in the Catholic tradition." It is important for the boards of such schools to understand that one cannot be both truly Catholic and completely independent. The ability of those governing a school to call it a "Catholic" school requires that the authority of the bishop, as outlined in Canon Law, be recognized. Before a decision to drop "Catholic" from a school's name is made, the ramifications of such a step should be seriously examined. There is no evidence to indicate that a civil court would allow a school or program to call itself "Catholic" in defiance of the diocesan bishop's directive.

The vast majority of religious education and youth ministry programs will be part of the juridic person of a parish. Campus ministers, for the most part, will be part of the Catholic high school.

Boards, Councils and other Advising/Governing Structures

Boards and their members have important responsibilities. It is crucial that board members understand that whatever power a board has, is vested in the board as a body, not in individual members. Board members must understand what the role of the board is—the development and/or recommendation of policy.

With the exception of high school boards and some regional school boards, the movement in the United States is toward advisory boards, rather than boards with specific jurisdiction. Advisory boards are consultative; their function is to give advice and offer consultation as requested; it is not to "govern" the school or program. The actions of an advisory/consultative board are subject to the decision of the pastor who has the authority to accept or decline the recommendations of the consultative board.

A board with limited jurisdiction is one that has been "constituted … to govern the parish education program, subject to certain decisions which are reserved to the pastor and the bishop" (CACE/NABE, p. 27). This type of board would have, in both theory and practice, more autonomy in decision-making than would the consultative board because decision-making powers have been delegated to the board. Whether a board is advisory or has limited jurisdiction, its role is defined by policy. Policy is usually defined as a guide for discretionary action. Policy will determine **what** the board wishes to be done. Policy is not concerned with administration or implementation; that is, the board should not become involved in **how** its directives will be implemented or *by whom* they will be carried out. For example, a board might adopt or recommend a policy requiring that the religious education program offer a First Communion preparation program for parents of First Communicants. The content and length of the program and the days on which it is to be offered are not the province of the board. Such questions are administrative ones; they are to be determined by the principal, DRE and pastor. Administrative decisions are the day-to-day management choices of the DRE, youth or campus minister. It is crucial that everyone understand these realities from the outset.

When tensions arise, as they almost inevitably do, board members must keep their responsibilities to the diocese and to the Church in view. Board members must be able to support the policies that are adopted; support does not necessarily mean agreement; support does mean a willingness to live with and not criticize the decision. If a person cannot support the policy, then change must be sought through the appropriate channels. If change cannot be achieved and the board member still cannot support the policy in question, then the person's only real choice is to resign from the board. The board member has to remember that the board's responsibilities are really two-fold: (1) to develop policies and (2) to support the persons and activities that implement those policies.

Disagreements should remain in the boardroom. Board members must remember that, as individuals, they have no real power. The power is vested in the board sitting as a body. Becoming involved in internal, administrative school conflicts only weakens the authority of both the board and the administrator. Board members have a right, however, to expect that the pastor and other administrators will keep them informed about problematic situations so that they will be able to respond intelligently if questioned. Since Canon Law governs the parish, school and their programs, board members and administrators have no authority to act outside the provisions of Canon Law. But within those provisions, boards have great freedom so long as no civil laws are broken. Both Canon Law and civil law provide boundaries for ministry.

Keeping Legally Sound Minutes

Board members, pastors, principals, DREs and youth/campus ministers often ask questions about the keeping of minutes: How do we best keep minutes? What should be in the minutes? Who should have access?

Many theories abound. Some persons advise recording everything that transpires in a meeting. Others advise writing as little as possible. Others suggest a compromise between the two positions. One reality is ever-present, however. What is written becomes a legal record and can be used both for and against the institution. Developing a planned, orderly, consistent approach to taking and keeping minutes is imperative.

Does State Law Govern Catholic Education/Ministry Board Meetings?

Catholic education and ministry boards govern private, not-for-profit, 501 (c) 3 organizations; as such, they are not generally subject to the same regulations as public organizations. Therefore, in the majority of cases, so-called sunshine laws requiring that meetings and the records of meetings be open to public scrutiny will not apply.

What Are Minutes?

Minutes are the written, legal record of actions taken at an official meeting of an official body. *Robert's Rules of Order*, the standard rule book for meeting process, states that the following should be included in minutes:

(1) the name of the organization (school board, parish council, parents' organization, etc.)
(2) the date of the meeting
(3) the place of the meeting (particularly if the meeting is held at a place other than the customary meeting place)
(4) presence of the regular presiding officer (president, principal, chair) and recording secretary or their substitutes
(5) names of members present and absent

(6) approval of the minutes of the last scheduled meeting of the board. (If the minutes are corrected, the corrections should be made in writing on the written minutes presented to the body for approval; new, corrected minutes should not be generated)

(7) officers and committee reports (the fact that a report was given is generally sufficient; the report can also be included as an attachment to the minutes)

(8) all motions including:
    (a) the name of the person who made the motion
    (b) the fact that the motion was the seconded (the name of the person seconding the motion is not absolutely required)
    (c) the complete text of the motion

(9) the vote on the motion:
    (a) the number of votes for and against
    (b) if a roll call vote is taken, the names of those voting for and against are documented

(10) any appeals or points of order taken (not an ordinary occurrence)

(11) beginning and ending times of the meeting.

How detailed should the minutes be?

Conventional wisdom suggests that less, rather than more, is the acceptable norm. Some attorneys in the not-for-profit arena advise: "Say as little as possible. Accurately record actions taken. Do not document discussion or who said what. Anything you write can be used against you in a court of law, especially when taken out of context."

How Should Executive Session Meetings be Documented?

An executive session occurs when the board determines that it will meet with only the members and guests invited for a specific reason, such as attorneys, in a confidential session. A wise course of action is only to record actions taken (motions passed). Much confidential information is often shared in executive sessions, such as personnel and financial information. The information and the discussion surrounding it should not be recorded in the minutes. Additionally, if legal counsel is present at an executive session, the attorney/client privilege may be lost if legal advice and discussion are recorded in the minutes.

Who Should Have Access to Minutes?

To a great extent, the answer to this question should be determined at the local level. Many parishes routinely publish the minutes of the parish council, for example, in the parish bulletin. Some schools and programs post the minutes of their board meetings on the parish or school web site.

Members of the board receive copies of the minutes. Policy should determine who else has access. A board might keep separate records of executive session meetings and not allow access to those records to anyone other than board members.

Some Do's and Don'ts for Keeping Minutes

(1) Do record only what must be recorded.

(2) Don't document discussion. Do record the names of those making motions or, if a roll call vote is taken, who voted for and against a particular motion.

(3) Do follow the rule, "Whatever is written should be specific, behaviorally-oriented and verifiable." Example: Mr. Jones made the following motion, "Catechists must complete the diocesan certification program within one year of their beginning service." After being seconded, the motion passed unanimously.

(4) Do enact a policy governing access to minutes.

(5) Keep an accurate, complete set of official minutes in a safe, secure place.

Protecting Board Members: Liability and Insurance Questions

Persons serving on boards often have questions concerning their personal civil liability if an individual should sue the board or its members. Historically, the doctrine of charitable immunity protected Catholic institutions and those persons associated with them; this doctrine has been generally abandoned. However, many states have passed laws that specifically protect members serving on boards of non-profit organizations, such as religiously-affiliated schools and programs, from civil liability. These laws presume *good faith* on the part of the board member; that is, a person is expected to act in the best interests of those served. Good faith is a traditional defense to most claims against board members in both the public and private sectors. Nonetheless, parishes and dioceses, as a matter of justice, should obtain and fund liability insurance for board members.

The best protection from a lawsuit is the effort to act always in accord with justice. The parish or sponsoring group should provide some in-service education in the legal aspects of board membership. The diocesan attorney will be able to provide information concerning the laws of a given state.

Chapter Five

Administrative Rights and Responsibilities

THE DRE, CAMPUS OR YOUTH MINISTER has the right and responsibility to administer his or her program. No one should interfere with that prerogative without serious cause. The DRE, for example, is entitled to the support of the bishop, the superintendent, the pastor and the board. If for sufficient reason, any one or more of those parties cannot support the DRE and an acceptable compromise cannot be reached, the DRE may have to leave the situation. Reasonable, good people can differ on how things should be done and a "parting of the ways" does not necessarily mean that one party is right and the other party is wrong. In any case, all parties have the obligation to support one another publicly and to address differences only in the appropriate forum.

Administrators have numerous responsibilities, many of which are not found enumerated in any document. The safest course of action for catechetical leaders and ministers is probably to assume that they are responsible for everything in their programs, unless responsibility for some aspect is clearly held by someone else. Much like the bishop and the pastor, the catechetical leader or youth/campus minister may delegate decision-making powers to other persons, but the responsibility cannot be delegated. If a lawsuit is brought against a parish or program, it is extremely likely that the administrator will be named as well.

Selecting Staff and Volunteers

The first task of most DREs and campus/youth ministers is recruiting, training and selecting volunteer staff. Virtually every ministerial program has them, even depends on them. Under the doctrine of *respondeat superior*, let the superior answer, the parish is responsible for the actions of its agents. Volunteers can be seen as agents. The 1997 Volunteer Protection Act was hailed as the federal government's way of ensuring volunteers in programs and institutions that needed them. State laws may also offer protection. What most people are not aware of, however, is that the protection is not absolute. It requires that a volunteer be immune from civil liability for any act or omission resulting in damages or injury. . .if the person was acting in good faith and within the scope of his official functions and duties, unless such damage or injury was caused by the willful or wanton misconduct of the person. It is easy to see that the protection contains a few holes—a litigant can always claim that the volunteer was acting in bad faith or that whatever was done was the result of misconduct. Even with liability possibilities, most parishes have a retinue of faithful volunteers. Because so many lawsuits today are alleging negligence on the part of volunteers, the following suggestions may be useful:

1. Understand what the Volunteer Protection Act and your state statute protect and what they do not protect.
2. Do not tell volunteers that they cannot be sued or that there is a law that does not allow people to sue them.
3. Follow reasonable procedures in the recruitment of volunteers. Be sure that all volunteers who work with minors have undergone a criminal background check.
4. Follow diocesan safe-environment policies and ensure that all volunteers complete mandated training.
5. If volunteers use their own vehicles in the performance of their duties, require that copies of their drivers' licenses and proofs of insurance be on file.
6. Provide a thorough orientation to volunteers.
7. Develop and disseminate a volunteer handbook.
8. Know what the institution's insurance covers and what it does not.
9. Remember—a volunteer can be "fired." It may be difficult, but sometimes it must be done for the greater good.

Administrators have two main legal responsibilities: (1) policy development—which most likely will be subject to review by a board, pastor or other party—and implementation of rules and policies and (2) supervision of staff, both paid and volunteer. Virtually every activity in which a program director engages can be placed under one of these two categories.

One of the administrator's most serious responsibilities is the supervision and evaluation of staff, both paid and volunteer. It is crucial that everyone understand that supervision and evaluation of personnel are the administrator's responsibilities. In reality, supervision is quality control for the program. It is far too easy to neglect supervision when one is confronted with numerous other administrative tasks. Many threats of lawsuits could be avoided if administrators simply followed existing policy and required staff to do the same.

Frequency and Format of Supervision

Administrators have a responsibility to supervise and evaluate staff. DRE supervision of catechists will likely be more structured and formal than a youth or campus minister's supervision of volunteers. Nonetheless, it must be done and documented.

If supervision is an ongoing, *formative* process, then both administrator and staff can grow together and help each other to improve the learning and/or ministerial environment. If supervision is viewed as punitive, as something that is only engaged in if the administrator is "out to get" someone, it will hardly be successful.

Evaluation is *summative*: an administrator sums up all the available data and makes a decision regarding contract renewal or continuation of volunteer activities. Evaluation then, should be based on more than supervisory data and should answer such questions as: Does this person support the rules of the program? Does he or she look after the safety of the children? Evaluation, then, is a broader concept than supervision, but both should be present in a good program.

All administrators must understand that paid and volunteer staff are present for the young people they serve; the young people are not there for adults' employment, self-fulfillment or service opportunities. Surely, there is no more sacred responsibility than ensuring that young people are being taught and formed by capable, competent, caring persons and that all are encouraged and given the means to become the best catechists and ministers possible.

Methods of Supervision

DREs may wish to use commercially available observation sheets when visiting classrooms or they may wish to develop their own. There appears to be no commercially available observation sheets for campus/youth ministers. However, ministers could develop a list of competencies, share that list with those who work in the ministry, and use that list as a basis for conversation. Perhaps, though, the best way is "management by walking around." If the DRE, youth or campus minister routinely walks through instruction and meeting areas, he or she will have a very good idea of what is going on and who needs help.

Dealing with the "problem" staff member or volunteer: creating a paper trail

Because religious education and campus/youth ministry programs routinely work with volunteers, it is easy to believe that one is fortunate to obtain whatever volunteers one can and that, in the absence of some outrageous behavior, volunteers cannot be fired. A volunteer can be terminated or told services are no longer needed. Such an action is not easy or comfortable, but sometimes it must be done. Prior to terminating or requesting a paid employee or volunteer to leave, the administrator should begin keeping a "paper trail" in the event the action is challenged legally or otherwise.

The administrator should document all events that illustrate what it is that makes the individual ineffective or undesirable in his or her role. Administrators should bear in mind that catechists may be doing an adequate job in the classroom, but may be behaving in ways that are unacceptable outside the classroom. Some examples might be excessive absenteeism, tardiness, lack of cooperation, failure to clearly uphold the teachings of the Church, etc. Documentation should describe behavior and avoid judgments. It would be better to record, "Mrs. Trapelo has missed three religious education classes in the last two months and failed to notify anyone. On four of the occasions she was present, she was at least fifteen minutes late" than to say, "Mrs. Trapelo is almost never here and she is always late. You can't count on her."

The following is a checklist for meeting with difficult volunteers and employees. It is similar to procedures used in many businesses. Following the steps can help to ensure that an appropriate documentation trail has been kept should administrative actions ever be challenged in court.

Points for Conferencing with Problem Employees and Volunteers

1. Enumerate precisely what is wrong and needs improvement.
2. State that you want the individual to improve.
3. State what the parish or school is going to do to help the individual.
4. Give a deadline at which time all parties will review improvement or lack of it.

5. Tell the person that, if there is no improvement within the time-frame stated, additional steps may be taken.
6. Give the person a copy of the conference document stating the first five points and ask him or her to comment on the document to ensure understanding.
7. Have the person sign the document and add any comments he or she wishes to include; if the individual refuses to sign, have another person present to witness the refusal.

Chapter Six

Parents and Young People:
Rights and Responsibilities:
What Do They Have a Right to Expect?
For What Are They Accountable?

T HE MOST BASIC RIGHT of parents and students in a Catholic program or school is the right to receive Catholic formation and education. The mission statement of the parish, school or program, the teachings of the Catholic Church and the Gospel should be the bases by which all actions are judged. Anything that interferes with formation and education should not be permitted, whether that interference originates with parents, staff, students or others.

Catechetical leaders, campus and youth ministers face the challenges of respecting the rights of young persons and parents while upholding discipline and order. Common law and common sense indicate that persons and institutions responsible for the education and formation of young people are expected to hold students to appropriate standards of behavior. Chapters I and II have discussed the fact that the main source of the law governing Catholic education and programs is contract law. The chapters also offered some information concerning the rights of those in the public sector. The wise administrator will be familiar with both the differences and similarities between the laws impacting them and those governing the public sector.

Student Rights

While Catholic institutions are not required to provide Constitutional due process protections, administrators are required to exercise fairness in their interactions with those served. At a minimum, as stated elsewhere in this text, a person accused of an infraction will be (1) told of the charges; (2) allowed to respond to them (3) before an impartial tribunal. The Gospel requires that parents and students be treated fairly in Catholic parishes, schools and programs. Fairness should be a goal of any institution purporting to prepare students for life. Deprivation of rights without at least the offer of an unbiased hearing before penalties are imposed is not fundamentally fair. Parents and young people have the right to demand fair treatment.

Although contract law is generally held to apply in cases involving Catholic schools and programs, courts historically have provided little protection on the basis of that law. That reality is beginning to change. As Catholic administrators require parents to sign statements that they have read and agree to be governed by the program handbook, so will courts require administrators to keep their "end of the bargain."

In the 1990s, courts seemed to disregard the doctrine of *in loco parentis*, schools and teachers stand "in the place of parents," which had previously been used to justify almost any action teachers took that a parent might take. In more recent times, however, the doctrine appears to have taken on new life. A sort of companion doctrine, *the fiduciary theory*, which holds that persons must take at least as much care of that which is entrusted to them as they would take if the entrusted entity were their own, has also arisen. Following this theory means that teachers and principals are expected to take care of their students in the same way they would care for their own children. The same theory, of course, can apply to any adult supervisors responsible for the welfare and instruction of young persons.

Most administrators and attorneys would agree that the best law is, like medicine, preventive. The best defense to a lawsuit is having tried to follow the right course in the first place. Administrators must realize that despite their best efforts in any and all areas, they may face lawsuits. All administrators must look carefully at their rules and procedures to ensure that they are reasonable, fair and consistent or else face the possibility of incurring problems and the expense of being sued.

It is the responsibility of the administrator to develop rules, promulgate them and supervise their implementation. A catechetical leader, youth or campus minister must be sure that students and parents know the rule and that staff is enforcing the rule. If through the negligence of staff or administration, students honestly do not know of a rule's existence, they can hardly be held accountable for not following the rule. If staff are responsible for the implementation of rules, it is important that they be supervised in the implementation of rules as well as in the delivery of instruction.

The importance courts rightfully place on the development, promulgation and implementation of rules is significant. Since handbooks and other written agreements can be construed as part of the contract existing between the parish, program or school, its students and their parents, it is important that, as far as possible and practical, rules be in writing.

Courts look for evidence of good faith: Did the institution have a rule? Was that rule promulgated? Did students and parents know of the rule? The court does not concern itself with the wisdom of the rule or even with the rightness or wrongness of the opinion of the rule-maker. Courts appear to be concerned only with the existence of a properly promulgated rule and with evidence that the institution acted in good faith according to the procedures it stated would be followed. Courts expect basic fairness in the execution of the contract between parent and parish, program or school when considering allegations that staff acted improperly in its imposition of disciplinary sanctions.

Administrators should understand that they will never be able to list every possible infraction a young person could commit. Therefore, it is advisable to have some type of "catch all" clauses such as "other inappropriate conduct" or "conduct, whether inside or outside the parish/program/school, that is detrimental to the reputation of the parish, program or school." Parents and young people need to understand that what a young person does, even if it occurs on his or her "own" time, outside the property, reflects on the parish, program or school. Parents should be helped to arrive at an understanding that their children are members of a faith and educational community and they have a responsibility to conduct themselves appropriately.

Recommendations for Rule Development

All Catholic schools, parishes and programs should develop clear rules governing behavior and clear procedures for dealing with misbehavior. Administrators must be concerned with being models of moral, ethical behavior; disciplinary policies and procedures must be examined in the light of Gospel principles and of the fundamental dignity that is the right of all persons.

The beginning point for the development of rules should be the parish/program/school's mission statement and philosophy. There should be a clearly written mission statement that informs all activities. The mission statement and philosophy must be viewed as living documents, not as something that was written once and put away somewhere to be brought out when the occasion requires it. If rules are clearly written, there is less likelihood that serious problems will arise when penalties are imposed. Whenever possible, rules should be written, a requirement supported by common sense reasons. It is easier to display the written rule when emotions run high than to insist that "at the beginning of the year, you were told about this rule."

Every parish, program and school should have a written parent/student handbook. Administrators should consider having parents and students sign a form stating that they have read the rules and agree to be governed by them. A written handbook should encourage administrators to strive for clarity in rule making. Periodic evaluation should enable the appropriate persons to make necessary changes in rules.

These recommendations may be helpful to Catholic administrators as they attempt to develop, modify and implement rules and policies. Ultimately, the guiding principle should be the desire to act in a reasonable, moral way consistent with the Gospel, one's philosophy and the principles of Canon Law.

The Rights of Parents

As most every educator would agree, parents are the primary educators of their children. They are the ones who should know the most about the children. In the best of all situations, parish, school and parents work together for the good of the child.

Parents have the right to expect that: (1) their children will receive what they are seeking—Catholic education and/or formation; (2) they will be able to present their concerns and discuss them in a respectful atmosphere; (3) they will receive timely responses to written requests and phone calls; (4) they will be encouraged to visit their children's classrooms and ministerial settings; (5) they will be notified of their children's progress or lack thereof; (6) their children will be treated fairly and (7) they will be promptly informed of any changes in rules and regulations.

Custody

Everyone who provides services for young persons that require supervision of children in the absence of the parents must remember that, unless altered by the court, both parents have rights. One cannot simply defer to the wishes of the parent one knows best or the parent one considers to be the more responsible individual. When a separation agreement is in place, a catechetical leader or minister can simply call the judge and ask for help. Parents can be required to furnish the school or parish with a court-certified copy of the custody section of the separation agreement or divorce decree. In the absence of any of the above, administrators must assume that both parents have custodial rights.

What does the law say about parents who are separated, but not yet divorced?

The law requires that each parent's rights be recognized. So, if a mother comes to the minister and states that she is going to leave her husband and she wants him to have no contact with the children, the minister or administrator must insist that a court-certified document be given to the parish or school which clearly states that the father is to be given no access to, and information concerning, his children before the wishes of the mother can be honored. While the rule of law is often clear, its application may be problematic. If a mother comes and states that she is terrified for her and her children's safety, the administrator must use common sense. No administrator who believes a mother's fear of abuse is going to release a child into the custody of the father without proper legal authorization. However, allegations of abuse can be made on both sides. In such situations, the administrator and/or pastor should contact local police and the diocesan or parish attorney. Child Protective Services may also be contacted. Once a separation or divorce decree is given, officials should comply with its directives.

What are a non-custodial parent's rights to access information about the child?

In the school setting, the Buckley Amendment provides clear guidelines governing access to academic-progress information. By extension, it seems best that administrators should follow the guidelines of the Buckley Amendment in dealing with non-school cases. The Buckley Amendment of 1975 clearly gives non-custodial parents rights in regard to the academic performance of their children. Unless a court has ruled otherwise, non-custodial parents have the right to copies of their children's records, although address and other identifying information can be excluded. The non-custodial parent also has a right to discuss his or her child's progress with school or program personnel. While a parish or school official may be required to provide access to each parent, it may not be necessary to hold duplicate conferences. The administrator may decide to require a joint conference. Caution is in order in such situations. If one parent has a restraining order against the other, a joint conference cannot be held.

Although it may be inconvenient to provide duplicate services, the educator or minister must keep in mind that the primary responsibility ethically, even if not absolutely legally required, is to protect the child and his or her interests. If a child's interests appear to be best served by separate conferences, the administrator should provide them.

How can I construct a policy that will govern custody situations?

One approach is to require that all separated and divorced parents provide the school or parish with a court-certified copy of the custody section of the appropriate decree. The custody section should provide information about the non-custodial parent's right of access to the child: For example, may the parent call for the child at school or at a parish program on the Fridays preceding weekend visitation?

All programs would be well-advised to gather as much data as possible concerning separated and divorced parents and their custodial rights and privileges, so that all will act in the best interests of the child and in a manner that is recognized by civil law.

Sacramental Preparation and Reception

While this is basically a topic concerning religious educators, there may be ramifications for other ministry programs. It is beyond the scope of this text to make suggestions concerning the content of sacramental preparation programs. A very difficult issue arises when a parent does not see that his or her child attends the religious education classes for First Communion preparation, but expects the child to make her First Communion with the other children. There are canonical issues here and the best action a director of religious education can take is to leave the matter to the decision of the pastor. It may be very difficult to watch a student who has not attended classes receive Communion, but Canon Law requires only that the person understand that Jesus is present in the Eucharist and be able to consume the wafer.

Confirmation poses different issues. A young person who does not wish to be confirmed should not be confirmed—even if he or she attended all the classes and fulfilled all the requirements of preparation. No parent can insist that a child be confirmed against the will of that child.

Prayer

Prayer is vitally important to the life of the Church and the lives of Church leaders. It is imperative that young people be encouraged to pray both individually and with the community. Those charged with the formation and education of persons must model fidelity to prayer.

Chapter Seven

Rights and Responsibilities of Staff

J ust as the rights of young people in Catholic schools and programs are significantly different than those of public school students, so, too, do the rights of catechists, ministers and volunteers differ from those of their public sector counterparts. Unless state action can be demonstrated, personnel can claim no protected activities under the Constitution and no due process protections under the Fifth and Fourteenth Amendments. Nonetheless, staff and volunteers do have rights. These are generally conferred by the contract or agreement existing between the parish, program or school and the staff person and so, the law of contracts can be invoked. Even if there is no salary involved, it is recommended that some sort of agreement, which clearly spells out duties, be signed. State and federal statutes confer other rights as well. Common law demands that persons treat other persons according to certain accepted standards of behavior.

Personnel Issues

Administrators must examine the legal soundness of actions and documents. Administrators should attempt to match their deeds with their words. Constraints, including financial ones, must be balanced against the requirements of justice. If an administrator moves outside the parameter of civil law, everything inside the parameter can be lost. Disagreements between personnel and officials cannot always be solved in the pastor's parlor. Regrettably, some disagreements propel the participants into court.

Subsidiarity and collegiality are values that should inform relationships and structures within the Church. *Subsidiarity* requires that persons having disagreements or complaints should seek discussion and resolution of the problem at the level closest to the problem. So, the catechist who has a disagreement with the DRE should not contact the pastor, board, or bishop before an attempt is made to resolve the matter with the DRE. If this process of subsidiarity became standard practice in Catholic formation and education, an untold number of problems might be solved before major crises develop, relationships rupture and lawsuits are filed. Of course, such principles are generally easier in theory than in practice.

Courts generally uphold personnel actions in Catholic programs and institutions because of the separation of church and state.

Employment Policies

Dioceses, parishes and schools are responsible for developing polices that protect the contractual rights of personnel. For example, a school has a contract with its teachers, and the faculty handbook can be considered part of the contract. Contracts place certain obligations upon teachers, but they also place obligations upon the employer. It is important that the diocesan and parish school's or program's policies be in line with those of the diocese, especially since most contracts bind the employee to observe the policies and regulations of the diocese.

Dioceses are certainly free to develop guidelines in addition to, or in place of, policies. Generally, a guideline allows more latitude on the part of the school than does a policy. However, dioceses should ensure that parishes, boards, pastors and principals understand what is intended by the guideline: How binding is it? Are certain guidelines more binding than others? In some dioceses, there are no educational policies per se—there are only guidelines. Diocesan personnel should be in contact with the bishop who, in terms of Canon Law, is the only lawgiver, to be sure that diocesan handbooks reflect his wishes and that all relevant parties are made aware of the binding power of policies.

Hiring policies are very important. Procedures must be in line with the requirements of civil law. Pre-employment inquiries carry the potential for violation of a person's rights. Administrators want to gather as much job-related information as possible, but at the same time invasion of privacy and discriminatory questions must be avoided.

Fidelity to Church Teaching

Today's Catholic educators talk a great deal about Catholic identity. What makes a school or program Catholic? How can a school or program and its staff claim its Catholic heritage? Does a catechist or minister have to agree with everything the Church says? What should a teacher say if a student asks for her opinion and she doesn't agree with the Church's position? Isn't it dishonest to support a position one thinks is wrong? These are all questions that most people will have heard. A Catholic school or program's first legal obligation is to be true to the teachings of the Catholic Church. No one is more important than the catechists and volunteers in ensuring Catholicity.

What Makes a Program Catholic?

Simply calling an institution or program Catholic does not make it so. Being Catholic requires a commitment to the Gospel, the teachings of Jesus Christ and the teachings of the Roman Catholic Church, both when it is convenient to be committed and when it is not so convenient. If any of the above are compromised, the school or program is eroding its Catholicity; one can legitimately argue that being Catholic is an either/or proposition: either the school is Catholic or it isn't.

"Cafeteria" Approaches to Catholicism Not Permitted

In the 1970s, many in the Church talked about a cafeteria approach to Catholicism: "I like the Church's teachings on social justice, so I'll support them. I think the Church is wrong about birth control, so I'll follow my conscience—after all, doesn't the Church teach that conscience is primary?" These statements are probably familiar to many people.

However, there is one basic requirement for all those representing the Catholic Church: to be true to the teachings of the Catholic Church. A Catholic educator or minister is an agent of the Catholic Church and has to hold the "company line," as it were. The situation is similar to that of any person who works for any organization.If an individual works for a company that makes umbrellas, he is expected to uphold the company's products. He probably won't be employed very long if he encourages people to buy plastic rain hoods as an alternative to umbrellas. Perhaps the analogy seems a bit simplistic, but the underlying premise is not: if one cannot support the company that one works for and the products the company produces, the honest course of action is to find another job. The product being "sold" is the Catholic faith. Parents send their children to Catholic schools for Catholic education and ministerial programs, not for the private opinions of staff members, and they have a legal right to expect fidelity to Church teaching.

Isn't Conscience Primary?

The Catholic Church does teach that one's conscience, properly formed, is primary. But the question of agency is still the "sticking point." If one teaches in a Catholic school and is asked about a matter concerning which he or she has a different personal position than the one the Church takes, the teacher is not at liberty to just share that opinion with students because he or she is an agent of the Church, the same way a bishop or the pope is an agent.

A recent Catholic school decision illustrates. In the 2004 case *Michele Curay-Cramer v. the Ursuline Academy of Wilmington, Delaware et al.*, a teacher signed an ad supporting a woman's right to choose to have an abortion. When school officials asked her to recant, she declined to do so. The school then terminated her employment. She brought suit alleging: gender discrimination, defamation, invasion of privacy, and tortuous interference with contractual relations. In dismissing the case, the judge ruled that such an application would violate the free exercise rights of the Catholic Church and, additionally, would constitute an impermissible entanglement of church and state.

So What's a Person to Do?

The Catholic educator or minister must present the teachings of the Catholic Church. It is certainly permissible to say that some persons do not agree with whatever the teaching is, but one must be clear about what the Church's position is. The educator is not free to say, for example, "I think the Church is wrong about birth control. Responsible persons use artificial contraception" or "Women should be ordained. The Pope is wrong." If pressed for a personal opinion, one can say, "My personal opinion is not what we are discussing. The Church teaches ..."

Sometimes, this reality is painful. The Church does not claim to be perfect, but persons who are responsible for the education and formation of young persons must teach them the precepts of the Church as the Church has taught them, not as individuals might like them to be. To do less is to fail in one's primary legal obligation.

Personal Conduct

Administrators are often faced with the issues of actual or perceived inappropriate staff conduct, and may wonder what legal rights they have in demanding certain standards of behavior from staff, particularly during off-campus times. What a staff member does, both in and outside the educational or ministerial setting, impacts the quality and integrity of ministry within the setting. The doctrine of separation of church and state protects administrators and allows them to set standards of personal behavior that would not be permitted in the public sector.

Behavioral Expectations for Catholic Educators and Ministers

Contracts and other documents governing employment and volunteer status should state that staff members are expected to support the teachings of the Catholic Church through their behavior. For example, if the fact that an individual had an abortion becomes known and is a source of scandal, the school and/or parish has every right to terminate that individual's employment or volunteer status. To do otherwise might send a confusing message to parents, students, and the larger community.

Issues of Sexual Preference and/or Lifestyle

Issues of sexual preference and lifestyle pose special problems. While no one should condemn a homosexual orientation, a Catholic administrator as an agent of the Church cannot ignore manifestations of an openly gay lifestyle that pose scandal. Persons of the opposite sex who are romantically involved and are living together, but not married, pose difficulties as well. The best approach may be to simply reiterate the Church's teaching that all sex outside marriage is wrong.

Equally difficult decisions must be made in situations involving divorced staff members who remarry without an annulment, if that fact becomes known. Even if the individual in question is convinced that he or she is acting in good conscience in contracting a second marriage, there is little doubt that the person is, objectively speaking, in violation of Church law and hence, a possible source of scandal. The situation is not a problem from the standpoint of terminating the employment of a person who violates Church law. Religious entities clearly can terminate the employment of one who violates religious norms. The problem is the lack of consistency from diocese to diocese, from parish to parish, and sometimes even within the same parish. All persons and institutions are expected to be fair. How can an employer claim to be fair in dealings with employees and volunteers if one is treated one way and a second person is treated another way for the same behavior, depending on who is involved? It is difficult to defend dismissal decisions on religious grounds if one person is dismissed for an action and another, having acted in the same manner, is retained. These principles hold in any case in which religious issues are involved. There is no easy solution but governing boards and administrators have an obligation to see that the teachings of the Catholic Church are respected and not compromised in the witness given by staff members. Many dioceses have policies that are concerned with scandalous public behavior.

In summary, then, once an individual performs an act that is inconsistent with Church teaching and that act becomes publicly known, the person may no longer be qualified to teach or minister at that time. While such a reality may seem obvious, it is recommended that documents state the requirement of supporting the teachings of the Church.

Illegal Activity

A person who has committed an illegal act may certainly have employment or volunteer status terminated. One who is convicted of, or who admits commission of, a crime should be removed from professional and/or volunteer status. The harder question arises when a person is simply accused of, or arrested on suspicion of, a crime. Administrators may be sharply divided as to the proper response to make in such a situation.

The United States has long operated under the principle of "innocent until proven guilty." It may appear that, until guilt is established, the fair approach would be to let the person continue in his or her position. Yet, the reality often is that effectiveness in such situations is severely compromised.

How, then, should one deal with an arrest of, or serious accusation concerning, a paid or volunteer staff member? Every parish and school should have a policy in place that allows the administrator to place the accused individual on a leave of absence pending the outcome of an investigation or an adjudication of guilt. The time to enact a policy is *not* when it is needed. The prudent administrator and board will have a policy in place that anticipates such situations. While realizing the complexity inherent in these situations, administrators must ensure that fidelity to the Church and compliance with law characterize policies and procedures; the member must support the teachings of the Catholic Church.

It seems that the safest legal course for schools and parishes to follow is to develop policy and to enforce it. As difficult as it may be to dismiss someone, it is unfair to pick and choose those who will be held to a policy. Justice demands that administrators construct policy that is applied equally to all.

Health Issues and the Law

Although persons in Catholic schools do not have the same Constitutional protections as those in the public sector, statutory laws such as health regulations can bind individuals in both the public and the private sector. Administrators should carefully read all health-related communications from state or local agencies. Administrators who should have known what the law was will be held to the same standard that persons who know the law are required to meet.

Planning

The first step in planning should be identification of any existing health or safety problems that can be remedied. Inviting everyone in the community to list problematic areas can aid in issue identification. Health and safety issues are related; failure to meet safety needs can result in health-related problems. A broken bleacher can result in a person's breaking a leg or arm. Courts expect that administrators will be proactive in identifying potential safety problems. At least once a year a complete safety audit of all buildings should be undertaken.

Staff Members and Health Issues

Staff members may be required to produce documentation of health and/or a doctor's statement that the person will not pose a health threat for the community. For example, tuberculosis, a communicable disease, poses a distinct threat. State law may require new teachers to have a tuberculin skin test and/or a chest X-ray to rule out the presence of tuberculosis before the teacher starts work. Catechetical leaders and campus/youth ministers may wish to enact a similar procedure.

Universal Precautions

Staff members should always use universal precautions whenever body fluids are present. If universal precautions are used, there is no reason for a supervising adult to refuse to deal with blood or other body fluids. No employee or volunteer dealing with children should be permitted to refuse to clean up body fluids or to render aid to a bleeding student. Clear procedures will help to ensure a calm, sound approach to situations involving body fluids.

The legal principle, often applied in negligence cases, "the younger the child chronologically or mentally, the greater the standard of care," applies in body fluid situations. Supervisors of small children are held to a higher standard; however, those who supervise older students are still held to the standard of taking whatever action a reasonable person would take.

Storing and Dispensing Medication

Every administrator has dealt, at one time or the other, with the problems of storing and dispensing student medication. In many elementary schools, a designated person such as the nurse or secretary may be responsible for medication storing and dispensing. In other schools, the task may be assigned to classroom teachers. High schools may expect students to be responsible for self-administering all medication.

Attorneys can identify problems with almost any approach. Whenever an educator or volunteer administers medication, he or she may be liable for any reaction which occurs. One dangerous policy allows parents to bring to the office over-the-counter medications with the young person's name written on them so that they can be stored and given as needed. The difficulty is that persons are having increasing problems with reactions to non-prescription medication, and a student could have a serious medical emergency after ingesting an over-the-counter medication. If parents are allowed to bring over-the-counter medication, the administrator should insist on written permission from both parent and physician.

The following statements offer some points to consider when policies and procedures are being determined.

1. The only persons who have an absolute right to the administration of medication are those who have serious chronic and/or life-threatening illnesses. For example, those who are allergic to bee stings must have the antidote serum readily available. A diabetic must be able to have prescribed insulin injections. Diabetics can, of course, be taught to administer and monitor their own medication; those allergic to bees most often need someone else to inject the antidote.

2. At least two persons must be identified who will be/are trained in the administration of injections or other drugs that a person cannot administer on his or her own.

3. Children and adolescents must be allowed to carry medication for life-threatening attacks. Asthma is one condition that may give no warning; if an inhaler is not immediately available, the student could be severely harmed.

4. Adults who administer medication must place their whole attention on the task. The proper paper-work should be present, e.g. a prescription label in the student's name, a doctor's note of authorization, and a parent's written permission.

5. If a teacher has a student with a life-threatening disease, the teacher must learn how to administer the medication. This reality is a matter of law, not choice.

6. Young children should not be responsible for oral medication, other than inhalers. Oral medication should be brought to and kept in the office.

7. High school-age persons may be allowed to carry and monitor their own non-prescription medication, so long as the parent/student handbook contains a statement to that effect.

Allergies and Allergic Reactions

Closely related to the question of medication is the issue of allergies and the school or program's responsibility to students with allergies. More students than ever have allergies and parents request administrators to:

(1) take appropriate measures to prevent exposure to allergens;

(2) keep and store medication;

(3) learn how to provide emergency medical treatment for allergic reactions; and

(4) educate young people and, indeed, the entire school community to the nature of allergic reactions.

Some staff members express fear or unwillingness to render aid to students experiencing allergic reactions. Teachers may ask if they "have to" assume such responsibility. Administrators may be concerned about liability.

Are students with allergies protected by disability law?

Yes. A disability can generally be defined as any condition that interferes with one or more life activities. Persons with certain food allergies or allergies to bee stings can experience life-threatening allergic reactions. Students with allergies may be considered as having disabilities covered by Section 504 of the Rehabilitation Act of 1973 (amended 1974) which prohibits educational programs receiving federal funds from discriminating against otherwise qualified students if, with reasonable accommodation, they can meet the school's requirements. Thus, students who need injections of adrenaline, for example, are protected. A student who cannot eat peanut butter or nuts is protected.

In 2004 the United States Office of Civil Rights held that a Brockton, Massachusetts Catholic elementary school violated Section 504 when it refused admission to a kindergarten child with a severe peanut allergy whose parents requested a peanut-free classroom. The school paid a settlement equal to the difference between its tuition and that of the private school the child attended. The Office of Civil Rights required that it monitor compliance for the following three years.

Must such students be admitted to Catholic schools and programs? Why?

Some school and diocesan administrators are receiving requests from parents of students who are not allergic to certain foods, such as peanuts, that students who are allergic not be allowed to enroll in the school. The request seems to stem from the school's limitation of types of snacks that can be brought to school for parties and sometimes what is served in the cafeteria. Since federal law protects such students, they cannot be refused admission simply on the basis of having an allergy that may inconvenience other students and/or their parents.

What about the rights of parents of students who are not allergic?
Can the school impose and must these parents follow restrictions because a few students have allergies?

Parents of non-allergic students must comply with school or program directives to refrain from sending snacks with peanuts or other allergens to their children's classes. They may have to accept that peanut butter or items with peanuts or items processed in plants where peanuts are processed may not be served in the cafeteria. These are simply reasonable accommodations. In one case, parents of one student with the peanut allergy requested that no one be allowed to bring peanut products of any kind into the school or program area. After consulting an attorney, the administrator asked the parents to produce a doctor's statement listing exactly what accommodations were necessary. A parent might believe that a child would be safest in a peanut-free environment, but if there is no medical necessity for that accommodation, the school is not obligated to make it. Thus, a school does not have to make every accommodation but only reasonable ones that are medically necessary. In one case, a student may need a completely peanut-free environment; in another environment, he or she may only need to avoid the allergen.

These situations present opportunities for compassion. In discussing restrictions with parents, administrators should stress not only the legal requirements but the Gospel imperatives of "loving one's neighbor as one's self" and the importance of "doing unto others as you would have them do unto you."

What are teachers and administrators required to do?

Teachers and administrators must do whatever is necessary to reasonably accommodate students with disabilities. A student must be allowed to carry an Epi-Pen if needed and the teacher must administer the injection if necessary. Failure to do so could result in serious injury to, or the death of, the student. Squeamishness must be set aside. Whatever a parent would reasonably do for a child, a teacher must do.

The following is a list of legal "do's and don'ts" when dealing with student allergies.

(1) Students cannot be refused admission or continued enrollment simply on the basis of their having allergies to food, insects or other substances.

(2) Reasonable accommodations must be made.

(3) If other students and parents are inconvenienced by the accommodations, they must accept the inconvenience.

(4) Educators must be willing to learn about the allergies and the treatment needed.

(5) Educators must be willing to administer medication when needed.

(6) Educators should not isolate such students or take actions that might separate the student from other students or activities without parental permission.

(7) Remind everyone that in every situation, all should act as Jesus would.

Chapter Eight

A Final Reflection: Is It Legal? Is It Ethical? Can I Do It? Should I Do It?

THIS TEXT HAS ATTEMPTED TO OUTLINE the provisions of civil law as they affect Catholic parishes, religious education, youth and campus ministry. The text offers suggestions that may be helpful as persons minister in the day-to-day world. This final chapter offers some thoughts for reflection.

One cannot simply ask, "Can I legally do this?" as a gauge for the rightness and wrongness of actions. Rather one must ask, "Looking at what the law requires and the Gospel demands, what should I do? What would Jesus do?" The latter are far more difficult questions than the first one and yet ministers and educators cannot simply consult legal texts or call lawyers for answers. Instead, all must search their hearts and consciences for the "right" answers and act accordingly.

The following quotation from T.S. Eliot's play, *Murder in the Cathedral*, sheds some poetic light on the subject: "The last temptation is the greatest treason; to do the right deed for the wrong reason." Not only must Catholic ministers and educators search for the "right" solutions to difficulties, they must search their motivations as well. For it is only when one is honest with one's self, that one can know the true peace of a decision well made.

Educators and ministers face complex situations that may seem to call for the wisdom of Solomon and the faith of a saint. Many crises do not fit into "textbook solutions." Civil law may allow one action but conscience may prescribe another path, one that is not simply legal but is also right. Just because the law allows an action does not mean the action is the right one to take. Decisions should not be made precipitously by one who is attempting to teach as Jesus did. Jesus did not shield persons from the consequences of their actions but did show mercy, an important point to remember when one is tempted to give up on an individual or situation.

A Model for Legal/Ethical Decision Making

It is easy to identify legal principles and judge past behavior on the basis of those principles. It is not so easy to decide what one ought to do in a present situation. The question should not be, "Is this what I can legally do?" but rather, "Is this what I should do?" One way to reflect on issues and decisions is to use a legal/ethical decision-making model. Six steps are suggested.

(1) Gather all relevant information.

Things are not always as they first appear. Facts are important, of course, but so are the reasons behind the facts. Is the problematic volunteer's spouse out of work? Is the troublesome student facing the loss of a parent due to divorce or illness?

(2) Identify legal issues.

If you are not sure of the issues, ask for help from the diocesan office or the parish attorney. Don't guess what the law might say. Get competent legal advice.

(3) Identify moral/ethical issues.

It is perfectly acceptable and not a sign of weakness to seek help in making this identification. Ask a peer what he or she sees as the issues or ask for a response on your own reading of the issues.

(4) List and consider possible courses of action.

Even if you are not sure that you would take a particular course of action, list it. Give yourself some time to consider the alternatives.Don't jump into action—if you can possibly wait.

(5) Ask yourself, "What would Jesus do?" This is not a quick, academic exercise. Pray and ask for guidance.

(6) Make your decision.

A Final Word

It can be very tempting to worry about legal issues and forget the rest. All of us who minister in Catholic education must remember that we are all part of the family of God. Those of us who have responsibility for the lives of others should always ask, "Is this the right thing to do? Are there less painful or difficult alternatives? How will I feel about this next year? In ten years? Is this the way I would want to be treated if I were in this situation? What would Jesus do?" On the Last Day, everyone will be required to account for decisions made and actions taken.

Appendix

Establishing Boundaries Between Catholic Memorial Employees/Volunteers and Students (Archdiocese Of Boston)

(Used with permission)

A s a school, Catholic Memorial wishes to encourage healthy relationships of mutual respect and trust between students, employees and volunteers. However, when dealing with students or recent graduates under the age of twenty-one, employees and volunteers must always conduct themselves in a manner that is above and beyond reapproach. Student safety is, and must be, paramount. When dealing with students and recent graduates under the age of twenty-one, employees and volunteers are required to conduct themselves in a manner that is always professional, avoiding all behavior and/or language that can violate the necessary, healthy distance that must be maintained at all times between adults and students.

As adults in positions of responsibility and authority, it is incumbent upon us to establish good boundaries with students. Good boundaries are the result of adult awareness and introspection. Good intentions are not enough to protect against the appearance of impropriety. As adults dealing with young people, we must ask ourselves not only, "What do I intend?" but "How might my words and actions appear to someone else?" When students address us with such titles as "Mr." or "Mrs." or "Brother" or "Coach" it should remind us that our relationships with students are *always* professional.

In light of this, the following policies must be strictly followed by Catholic Memorial employees and volunteers when dealing with Catholic Memorial students and recent Catholic Memorial graduates under the age of twenty-one. Numbers 1 through 6 require specific approval by the President/Principal or their designee:

1. Off-campus contact that is school-sponsored or school-sanctioned must always be treated as a school field trip. With the exception of normally scheduled athletic practices or competitions, all such activities require parental permission in writing (fax or e-mail is acceptable).

2. No Catholic Memorial student or recent graduate under the age of twenty-one is allowed into the home or vehicle of a Catholic Memorial employee or volunteer without the expressed permission of the student's parents or guardians.

3. Employees and volunteers may not socialize or meet off-campus with Catholic Memorial students or graduates under the age of twenty-one unless the parent or guardian has given expressed permission for the meeting or is present.

4. Employees and volunteers are not permitted to provide professional services (i.e. tutoring, counseling, legal, physical condition/therapy) outside of the regular terms of employment to Catholic Memorial students or recent graduates under the age of twenty-one.

5. Employees and volunteers are not permitted to hire for any personal purpose Catholic Memorial students or recent graduates under the age of twenty-one. Similarly, employees are not permitted to accept student "volunteers" for personal needs, services or projects.

6. Outside of regular school hours or regularly defined duties, employees and volunteers are not to meet privately at Catholic Memorial with Catholic Memorial students or graduates under the age of twenty-one.

7. Electronic communication between students and employees/volunteers is only permitted through the Catholic Memorial e-mail system and/or websites hosted by Catholic Memorial.

8. When contacting a student at home, every attempt must be made to speak with the parent/guardian as well.

9. Employees and volunteers must never discuss with Catholic Memorial students or recent graduates under the age of twenty-one the problems, deficiencies or challenges of any school employee or Catholic Memorial student unless that person's well being is in question.

10. With regard to issues of confidentiality, employees and volunteers are to offer a disclaimer for Catholic Memorial student confidence: "I can keep confidence only if it is about something not harmful to you or others."

11. Employees and volunteers must not share intimate, personal and/or family information with Catholic Memorial students. In addition, employees and volunteers should not give personal phone numbers or personal e-mail addresses to Catholic Memorial students.

12. Employees and volunteers must not permit and/or join in any bullying of Catholic Memorial students. Employees are obliged to stop bullying and to admonish student(s) that such behavior is unacceptable.

13. Employees and volunteers should never tease students, adopt a deriding, sarcastic tone, or use racial, sexual, vulgar or provocative language. Such behavior has no place in our school and runs counter to our school values and philosophy.

14. Employees should never threaten students with secrecy such as, "this must stay in the classroom/locker room," or "I am only going to tell you this but you can't tell your parents," etc.

Catholic Memorial takes seriously its moral and legal obligation to protect students from physical and sexual abuse. All allegations of employee or volunteer impropriety involving Catholic Memorial students or recent Catholic Memorial graduates under the age of twenty-one will be thoroughly investigated.

Glossary Of Terms

Board

A board (committee/council/commission) is a body whose members are selected or elected to participate in educational decision-making at the diocesan, regional, inter-parish or parish level.

Board with Limited Jurisdiction

A board with limited jurisdiction has power limited to certain areas of educational concern. It has final, but not total, jurisdiction in certain areas.

Collegiality

Collegiality is the sharing of responsibility and authority. In the Catholic Church, bishops have the highest authority within a diocese. Powers may be delegated to other parties, such as boards.

Common Law

Common law is that law not created by a legislature. It includes principles of action based on long-established standards of reasonable conduct and on court judgments affirming such standards. It is sometime called "judge-made law."

Compelling State Interest

Compelling state interest is the overwhelming or serious need for governmental action. The government is said to have a compelling state interest in anti-discrimination legislation and in the elimination of unequal treatment of citizens.

Consultative (advisory) Board

A consultative board is one which cooperates in the policy-making process by formulating and adapting, but never enacting, policy.

Contract

A contract is an agreement between two parties. The essentials of a contract are: (1) mutual assent (2) by legally competent parties (3) for consideration (4) to subject matter that is legal and (5) in a form of agreement that is legal.

Defamation

Defamation is an unprivileged communication. It can be either spoken (slander) or written (libel.)

Due Process (constitutional)

Due process is fundamental fairness under the law. There are two types:

Substantive Due Process: "The constitutional guarantee that no person shall be arbitrarily deprived of his life, liberty, or property; the essence of substantive due process is protection from arbitrary unreasonable action" *(Black's Law Dictionary).* Substantive due process concerns *what* is done as distinguished from *how* it is done (procedural due process).

Procedural Due Process: how the process of depriving someone of something is carried out; *how* it is done. The minimum requirements of Constitutional due process are *notice* and a hearing before an *impartial tribunal.*

Fiduciary

A fiduciary is one who has accepted the responsibility for the care of people or property.

Foreseeability

Foreseeability is the "the reasonable anticipation that harm or injury is the likely result of acts or omission" *(Black's Law Dictionary).* It is not necessary that a person anticipate the particular injury that might result from an action, but only that danger or harm in general might result.

Invasion of Privacy

Invasion of privacy is a tort action in which the plaintiff alleges that the defendant has unreasonably invaded personal privacy, e.g., revealing confidential information in student or personal files without the individual's consent.

Judicial Restraint

Judicial restraint is the doctrine that courts will not interfere in decisions made by professionals.

Negligence

Negligence is the absence of the degree of care which a reasonable person would be expected to use in a given situation. Legal negligence requires the presence of four elements: duty, violation of duty, proximate cause, and injury.

Policy

A policy is a guide for discretionary action. Policy states *what* is to be done, not *how* it is to be done.

Proximate Cause

Proximate cause is a contributing factor to an injury. The injury was the result of or reasonably foreseeable outcome of the action or inaction said to be the proximate cause.

State Action

State action is the presence of the government in an activity to such a degree that the activity may be considered to be that of the government.

Tort

A tort is a civil or private wrong as distinguished from a crime.

Bibliography

Bischoff v. Brothers of the Sacred Heart, La. App. 416 So. 2d 348 (1982).

Black, Henry Campbell. *Black's Law Dictionary* (5th ed.) St. Paul: West, 1979.

Bob Jones v. United States, 103 S.Ct. 2017 (1983).

Brooks v. Logan and Joint District No. 2 903 P.2d 73 (1995).

Buckley Amendment of 1975.

CACE/NABE Governance Task Force. *A Primer on Educational Governance in the Catholic Church*. Washington, D.C.: NCEA, 1987.

Caston v. Buckeye Insurance Company (1982) 8 Ohio App.3d 309.

Civil Rights Act of 1964.

Copyright Act of 1976.

Curay-Cramer v. The Ursuline Academy of Wilmington, Delaware, Inc., et al., C.A. No. 03-1014-KAJ (November 16, 2004).

Davis v. Homestead Farms, 359 N.W.2d 1.

Encyclopedia Brittanica v. Crooks, 542 F. Supp. 1156 (W.D.N.Y. 1982).

Franklin v. Gwinett County Public Schools (1992), 530 U.S. 60.

Gatti, Richard D. and Gatti, Daniel J. *New Encyclopedic Dictionary of School Law*. West Nyak, NY: Parker, 1983.

Geraci v. St. Xavier High School, 12 Ohio Op. 3d 146 (Ohio, 1978).

Gorman v. St. Raphael Academy, Sup. Ct. (R.I.) No. 2003-371-Appeal (PC01-4821, July 15, 2004).

"Guidelines for Classroom Copying in Not-for-Profit Educational Institutes," House Report 94-1476, 94th Congress 2d Session (1976).

"Guidelines for Off-Air Recording of Broadcast Programming for Educational Purposes," CONG. REC.E4750 (daily edition October 14, 1981).

Holy Names v. Retlick (1983) 326 N.W.2d 121 (Wis. App.).

Immediato v. Rye Neck School District (1996), 73 F.3d 454 (2d Cir.), cert. Den., 117 S.Ct. 60.

Individuals with Disabilities in Education Act (1997).

Ingraham v. Wright (1977), 430 U.S.65.

Keiser v. Catholic Diocese of Shreveport, Inc., Ct. of Appeals, 2d Circ., No. 38, 797 CA (Louisiana, 2004).

Levandowski v. Jackson City School District, 328 S.2d 339 (Minn. 1976).

Little v. St. Mary Magdalene, 739 F.Supp. 1003 (1990).

Maracallo v. BOE of City of New York, 769 N.Y.S.2d 7171 (Sup. 2003).

Marcus v. Rowley (1983), 695 F.2d 1171 (9th Cir.).

Merickel, Mark. "The Educator's Rights to Fair Use of Copyrighted Work." West's Education Law Reporter 51 (3) 711-724.

New Jersey v. T.L.O., 105 S. Ct. 733 (1985).

Pastoral Statement of U.S. Catholic Bishops on Handicapped People. Washington, DC: United States Catholic Conference,1978.

Reardon v. LeMoyne et al., 454 A.2d 428 (N.H. 1982).

Robert, Henry M. III et al. Robert's Rules of Order (10th ed). Cambridge, MA: Perseus, 2000.

Roy v. Columbia Broadcasting System (1979). 503 F.Supp. 1137 (S. D.N.Y. 1979).

Section 504 of the Rehabilatation Act of 1973 (amended 1974).

Smith v. Archbishop of St. Louis, 632 S.W.2d 516 (1982).

Tinker v. Des Moines Independent Community School District et al., 393 U.S. 503 (1969).

Titus v. Lindberg, 228 A.2d 65 (N.J., 1967).

United States Code Annotated.

United States Constitution.

Weithoff v. St. Veronica's School, 210 N.W.2d 108 (Mich. 1973).

About the Author

Sister Mary Angela Shaughnessy, SCN, J.D., Ph.D.

Sister Mary Angela Shaughnessy is a Sister of Charity of Nazareth who has taught at all levels of Catholic education from elementary through graduate school. She served eight years as principal of a Catholic high school. Sister Mary Angela holds a bachelor's degree in English, a master's degree in English, a master's degree in educational administration, a J.D. degree in law and a Ph.D. in educational administration and supervision. Her research centers on the law as it affects Catholic education and Church ministry. She is the author of more than thirty texts.

A consultant to numerous dioceses, Sister Mary Angela is a regular speaker at the NCEA conventions. Sister has served as adjunct professor in various college and university programs. She has served as visiting professor at the University of San Francisco since 1988. Sister Mary Angela has held various administrative posts in higher education. Currently, she is professor of education at Spalding University in Louisville, Kentucky. Additionally she is executive director of the Education Law Institute. Sister is the recipient of numerous awards. In 1997 she was named one of the 25 most influential persons in Catholic education.